Kate

Hope it holds your
interest.

Alan

Cult of the Imaginary Circle

Akmed Khalifa

Copyright © 2005 by Akmed Khalifa

Cult Of The Imaginary Circle

All rights reserved. No part of this book may be reproduced or transmitted in any form or by any means. Electronic, or mechanical, including photocopying, recording or by any information storage and retrieval system, without permission in writing from the publisher. No abridgement or changes to the text are authorized by the publisher.

Published by It Is Written Publishing Company, a division of It Is Written Bookstore, Inc.

It Is Written Publishing
10819 Wyndham Pointe Drive
Charlotte, NC 28213

Ordering Information:
ISBN 159712-012-X
http//www.itiswrittenbookstore.com

Library of Congress Cataloging-in-Publication Data
Akmed Khalifa

Printed in the United States of America

Table of Contents

Prologue i

Acknowledgements iii

Dedication v

CHAPTER 1 1
"The Gitty Up"

CHAPTER 2 7
"No Home like Homewood"

CHAPTER 3 19
"In the Circle in The Room"

CHAPTER 4 27
"Cult Tradition"

CHAPTER 5 35
"Scrub Life"

CHAPTER 6 43
"Malcontents"

CHAPTER 7 51
"Gain from Pain"

CHAPTER 8 57
"The Two-Helmet Meeting"

CHAPTER 9 65
"A Turn for Champions"

CHAPTER 10 "Fate Twists"..73

CHAPTER 11 85
"Fixed, Frozen, Shocked"

CHAPTER 12 97
"One Day…and It Won't Be Long"

EPILOGUE 113

ABOUT THE AUTHOR..117

Prologue

Cult Of The Imaginary Circle is a gripping true story of how institutionalized violence controlled the lives of teenaged boys in the African American community of Homewood in Pittsburgh, Pennsylvania. Set in the 1960s, it is replete with examples of the cultural dynamism that were found in the hip East Coast urban communities of the era.

This book reveals how the ritualistic, cult-like behavior of the legendary Westinghouse Bulldogs was responsible for the degradation and the exaltation of individual team members and the collective spirit of the team. It is told from the perspective of an insider, a participant, a devotee of the culture and the traditions. A frightening tradition, "The Room", began in the early 1950s and continued into the late 1990s.

The story is told through my life and is a coming-of-age tale of struggle and triumph. The reality of this history, although known by many members of the Homewood community, has never been told publicly, openly discussed, or exposed to any significant degree. Yet it is an important story to tell because it provides insight into why inner-city youths become members of violent gangs and why the practice of hazing is still popular among young people today.

Cult Of The Imaginary Circle is a view of the inner sanctum of one of the most successful high school football teams in the country. No names have been changed. What you are about to read is my recollection of the facts and circumstances and the real people who created them.

Akmed Khalifa (Frank Reed)

Acknowledgements

Many thanks to Alfred Babington-Johnson, Menia Buckner, and Vera Lige for listening to my story and inspiring me. Many thanks to Joe Avent, Wes Garnett, Leo Loar, Art Davis, and Clifford Walker for fill-in on some of the details; and thanks also to Ross Plaetzer.

A huge debt of gratitude is owed to my sister Janet Reed for editing this work.

Dedication

TO ALL THOSE SCRUBS WHO ENDURED FOR

THE LOVE OF THE GAME

CHAPTER 1

"The Gitty Up"

There we were, on a raggedy, rickety old bike poised for a wild ride down one of the most treacherous hills in Homewood. Brushton Avenue was long and steep with a couple of hellacious turns so sharp that you couldn't see approaching traffic beyond the wide bends, traffic notorious for speed and disregard for anyone or anything in its way.

Of course that didn't matter. Nor did it matter that my parents had warned me dozens of times about the dangers of bike riding down the unsafe and mind-boggling hills of Pittsburgh. It didn't matter that one of my friends had been killed just walking his bike across the street. It didn't matter that my parents refused to buy me a bike and had actually forbidden me from riding one.

So, there we were, at the top of Brushton Avenue, with my cousin Butch Reed at the handle bars and me sitting on the back of this bike held together with wire, tape, and divine thread. I was holding on to the back of the frame with one hand and a rusty old tire pump with the other. There were so many holes in the tires that we had to pump them up every ten minutes or so. All of that not withstanding, Butch yelled, "You ready?"

"We ain't gone yet?" I replied, and down we plunged.

We went from zero to too fast in a pair of seconds, quickly past gap-mouthed friends and pointed fingers of concerned neighbors. Hard jutting cobblestones jostled us through the first turn like a runaway roller coaster racing over speed bumps. I held onto the back of the bike so tightly that I could feel the paint sticking to my fingers. As we leaned to the right coming out of the first bend, a rocket 88 Oldsmobile flew past us followed by three or four vehicular blurs sucked up in its exhaust.

Heading into the second straightaway, where we could see approaching traffic, we took the middle of the hill at breakneck speed, faster than I thought possible on that rickety rack of tin we were riding on. We were coming to the final curve before the last long straight away that led to the intersection of Brushton and Frankstowne Avenues, famous for bone-crushing, metal-twisting accidents.

"Slow down," I yelled. "We're near Frankstowne."

"I can't, the brakes don't work," Butch hollered back. Panic quickly found its way to the back of the soon-to-be-unoccupied bike frame. Every kid in Homewood was terrified of biking through the Brushton and Frankstowne intersection and I was no exception. We were about to pass Ruby's, a small corner grocery store, when I decided to exit the rear of the bike. I pushed off of the frame with one hand and attempted to land on my feet.

As I opened my eyes, tiny little stars circled my vision. I was looking up at a crowd of people hovering over me on the sidewalk in front of Ruby's store. I had been roughly bounced from the middle of the street like a poorly tossed football and landed on my back on the sidewalk. I could faintly hear murmuring voices swirling above me. In the fraction of a second, in the foggy stream between consciousness and unconsciousness, during that drowsy drift, something strange happened, truly an otherly thing took place: my first contact with The Cult of the Imaginary Circle. All I could see was a blur of blue and gold above me. I was sliding in and out of someplace I had never been before. Then I felt what seemed like a hand pulling at the front of my shirt and I heard a compelling voice say, "Get up, get up. Ain't nothin' wrong with you."

I struggled to my feet, assisted by my cousin but the blur of blue and gold had vanished along with the voice that had brought me back to consciousness.

"Hey man, you all right?" Butch asked.

"Yeah, I said. "How did you get off the bike?" At that point, he fell down laughing. I looked over at the side of Ruby's store and leaned up against the wall was the bike, in no worse shape than when we began our descent. "How'd you stop the bike?" I asked. In between pure fits of laughter he told me that the brakes were okay; he was just playing when he said they weren't working. Immediately, I jumped on top of him and started punching him. This made Butch laugh even more, and soon we were both laughing uncontrollably as I put him in a headlock and wrestled him to the sidewalk.

As we made our way back up the hill, I couldn't believe what had just happened. I asked Butch about the guy in the blue and gold who pulled me up from the sidewalk.

"Who?" He asked.

"The guy in the blue and gold," I said.

"Man, that must'a been a dream, he said. "There wasn't nobody in blue and gold. I helped you up from the sidewalk."

"Yeah, you helped me down, too," I said, which launched him into another laughing fit, and I pummeled him with my fists again and we laughed and fought all the way home.

Nursing the scratches and bruises on my knee and arm, I vowed never to ride a bike down Brushton Avenue again. I waved to Butch as he headed home, down the sidewalk this time, a little late for caution I thought as the knot on the back of my head grew to the size of a small apple. I decided if asked about my injuries that I would say without further clarification that I fell running down the steps in front of our house. As I slid across the chairs at the dinner table I kept my bruised arm hidden under the table and was careful to keep the back of my head out of

3

clear view. It was an uneventful meal with my two older sisters, Janet and Ann, chattering back and forth in between my parents' conversation about the health and wealth of our hillside community.

After dinner, my family seemed a little surprised when I said I was going to bed early because I was sleepy. I was always the one who had to be forced to go to bed after falling asleep on the living room floor. "I'm just restin my eyes," I would exclaim as they would nudge me awake. I slowly climbed the sixteen steps to our second floor in what I thought was a big, spooky old house at times, particularly when I was alone and especially at night. Each step had its own creak, a creepy yet comforting reality because it was impossible for anyone to sneak upstairs without being heard. Our house had seven rooms: three bedrooms and a bathroom upstairs and a living room, dining room, and kitchen downstairs. Then there was the basement.

The basement, was the creepiest place in the house, literally a scene out of a ghost story or monster movie. There was a big locking trap door over the nine steps leading down into the basement, which made it even scarier. Why would it need to be locked if there were nothing down there that had to be kept from coming upstairs? There was one light in the basement, right in the middle of the room, which had to pulled on by the chain hanging from the socket, a fact that meant never go down in the basement alone at night. But I had my method for going down there when I was forced to. I would cling to the side of the wall as I stealthily inched down the steps. Once on the bottom step, I furiously punched and kicked my way to the light socket chain, figuring that if there were someone or something down there, I would get it before it got me. The basement was the home of big hairy spiders and big spider webs that I would occasionally fight my way into and get a face full of. I often had to stoke the big coal-burning furnace that sat adjacent to the coal bin, another even creepier place with a big wooden bar across the door; a bar that often was left leaning up against the wall, which meant the accursed coal bin was unlocked.

Meanwhile, I reached the top step to the second floor and made my way back to my bedroom and decided to take a bath before going to bed. I locked the bathroom door, ran some bath water and climbed into the tub. Soon there was a knock on the bathroom door.

"Boy are you sick?" my mother yelled.

"Open this door, there must be something wrong with you," my father said. Going to bed early was one thing, but taking a bath without being told was contradictory to legends of dirty, stinky little boys climbing into bed without bathing.

Exchanging laughter and disbelief, my family trucked back downstairs. "Don't forget to clean out the tub," my mother yelled.

"I won't," I asserted and simultaneously as if rehearsed, my sisters added, "And don't leave your clothes all over the floor either."

"Oh shut up," I replied as I rinsed the soap from my face and prepared to exit the tub. Piling my clothes on the chair in my room, I climbed into bed and, forgetting about the knot on my noggin, reclined on my back. When my head hit the pillow, I was painfully reminded of the protrusion on the back of my head, and I quickly flipped to my right side.

The bruise on my right arm however, forced me to commit to the left side of my body for painless repose.

I slowly drifted off to a fitful sleep wherein I relived the day's episode of downhill racing. In one of the night's many dreams, a strange blue and gold mist reminiscent of what I saw as I peered up from the sidewalk of Ruby's store appeared to hover over my bed. I was both afraid and comforted, at once challenged and empowered. Little did I know what it meant nor why it had chosen to represent itself to me twice in one day, but it was truly a harbinger of things to come from The Cult of the Imaginary Circle.

CHAPTER 2

"No Home like Homewood"

Early sunlight filling my bedroom and penetrating my eyelids awakened me. It was Saturday morning and my opportunity to make some money. I grabbed the pile of clothes on the chair in my room and on my way past the dirty clothes hamper at the top of the steps, deposited them with a right-hand stuff. I reached for the banister with my left hand and jumped down the steps four at a time into the kitchen. I poured some cereal in a bowl and reached in the cupboard for a can of evaporated milk. I mixed a half of a glass of it with a half of a glass of water and poured it over the cereal. We rarely had whole milk and, as quiet as it was kept, we didn't miss it. Several quick spoonfuls later, I was tugging at my Radio Flyer wagon preparing for a ride down the sidewalk of Hermitage Street en route to the A&P grocery store. There, I would make a few coins helping elderly women get their groceries home.

I pulled my wagon across Brushton Avenue onto Hermitage Street. Hermitage began at Brushton and, for a block, was a fairly steep incline. As I got ready to ride down the sidewalk, I loaded my wagon with several sizeable rocks; ammunition to hurl at one of the dirty, mangy neighborhood dogs that would chase anyone riding anything down the block for a chance to bite at their feet. Sure enough, as I began my descent, this fool dog emerged from behind a tree across the street, appearing to lick his chops. He charged across the cobblestones toward me growling, showing his rotting canine teeth. It was either outrun him or fend him off with a barrage of rocks. I reached into my wagon as I rolled downward, grabbed a medium sized rock and fired it at this menacing alley dog that had me in its sights. That one missed, and undaunted, he continued his charge. He was running at me like a defensive safety angling toward a halfback headed for the goal line on a football field. I reached into my wagon again for another rock, retrieved a sizable chunk of chipped sidewalk and sent it airmail toward my approaching nemesis. The chunk of concrete hit the street in front of him breaking into several pieces, one of which hit him dead on the nose, stopping him dead in his tracks. Rid of him, I breezed down the sidewalk, continuing my Saturday morning adventure.

Once I turned the corner onto Homewood Avenue, it was a different scene altogether. Clearly, I had stepped into the business hub of the community and on the busiest day of the week. The sidewalks were full of people scurrying in and out of shops lining both sides of the street. Extraordinary conversation filled the early morning air as hundreds of feet pounded the pavement. Car doors slammed and car horns honked. Coins jingled and crisp paper bags scrunched and crunched in the arms of busy shoppers. The smell of fresh baked goods from the bakery watered my mouth in anticipation of hand-sized jelly donuts and chewy chocolate chip cookies. I weaved my way down the sidewalk in and out of the crowd of avenue patrons and parallel parked my wagon under the window in front of the A&P.

A pocketful of change and a handful of chocolate chip cookies later, I headed home to spend the rest of the day playing with my friends. After checking in with my family and stashing my coins, I bounded outside and onto the steps in front of our house.

The concrete steps were bordered on both sides by green tubular metal railings, great for climbing on and sliding down. The city steps, which loomed large for a kid of my age, ascended the hillside in front of our house and disappeared into the visible horizon.

I climbed onto the top of one of the railings and, as I slid down sideways, noticed two strange pieces of wood sticking out from under a portion of the steps. I climbed over the side of the railing and jumped down into the weeds to see what they were. I grabbed the ends and tugged away until it was evident that they were the ends of an old ladder someone had ditched. It was a rather long ladder, full of splinters and with more than a few rungs missing. In fact there were only four rungs still intact. "Perfect," I thought. I hollered across the street to Bucky who was sitting on the curb in front of his house.

"Hey man, come see what I found under the steps," I yelled.

"What is it?" he asked as he ran across the street and up the steps.

"It's a old ladder," I told him as I struggled to dislodge it. He stood with a puzzled look on his face as he tried to figure out what on earth we could do with such a raggedy piece of abandoned junk. But when I told him that it was perfect for riding down the steps and that it had a front and back seat with foot pedals his eyes lit up at the possibilities.

Soon, we had freed our new ride and were headed up the steps for a trial run. Any trek up the steps came with serious cause for concern. To get to the top, you had to go past Miss Thompson's house and past her yard occupied by the scariest dogs in the community. Rumor had it that she fed them gunpowder to make them mean, and they were very mean and very scary. The fact that she kept them chained to the side of her house was of little consolation to passersby. Whenever anyone got to within ten feet of the landing in front of her house, rustling chains and ferocious barking warned of imminent danger. Anyone continuing up the steps was then treated to choking growls as these beasts strained against the chains pulling at their necks. Standing on their hind legs and clawing at the air, they bared huge canine teeth awash in saliva. There was never any doubt as to why there was a clear path through the weeds on the other side of the concrete landing across from her yard. A couple of extra feet away from the frothing hillside creatures was a measure of comfort most people took advantage of.

Miss Thompson was a legendary figure in the community. She was in her seventies but was fit as a fiddle. She looked like she could have been a mixture of African American and Native American heritage. She had straight black hair with a long bang across her forehead, and she was thin and wirery with dark skin. Her arms were thin but muscular, with many thick veins running from her elbows to the knuckles on her strong, callused hands. She lived alone and had a reputation for being very tough and fearless.

One story about her told of how there had been a spate of purse snatching in the community and no one had been caught and prosecuted. The perpetrators usually picked older, more vulnerable women to rob, until the day one of them attempted to snatch Miss Thompson's purse and run. It had been a warm day and in the early evening Miss Thompson was walking up Brushton Avenue with her purse over her left shoulder and a brown paper bag in her right hand. A young thug approached her from behind and, when he got to within ten feet of her, began to run. She must have heard his quickening footsteps because she tightened the grip on her purse strap.

When he was even on the sidewalk with Miss Thompson, he reached out to grab her purse strap and run by her. The strap slid off of her shoulder but went no further than her left hand. She yanked at the strap and pulled the purse and the surprised perpetrator back toward her. Unbeknownst to the would-be thief, Miss Thompson had a hammer concealed in the brown paper bag in her right hand and she swung it with pinpoint accuracy to the top of his head. Womp! She found pay dirt not once but twice as she bounced the hammer-laden brown paper bag off his cranium. As his knees buckled, he lost his grip on the purse and fell to the ground. Miss Thompson stood over him while he writhed in pain on the sidewalk and in a stern voice said, "Now, young man, find some work and leave us old ladies alone."

She situated her purse back over her shoulder and continued back up the hill as if what had just happened was of little consequence. Although she had a tough reputation she was good people, salt of the earth. She was kind and considerate and would do anything for you within her abilities, just as long as you didn't try to take advantage of her.

Nevertheless, her hellhounds were not enough to deter us from carrying our newly acquired vehicle past her house to position it for a ride down the steps. They lunged ferociously as we charged past them laughing, yet cautiously keeping the ladder between them and us. Reaching the top of the steps, we put the ladder down and climbed aboard. I sat at the front of the ladder, stretched my feet out to the front rung while Bucky sat at the back and put his feet on the last available rung. Placing our hands down on the steps, we pushed off and began the first short slide. We went down only a couple of steps and stopped suddenly. We hadn't pushed hard enough, and we backed up for another try. This time we, bumped down a whole flight of steps, sliding off sideways into the weeds. We picked up our ride and carried it over to the next landing to an awaiting flight of steps and pushed off again, managing to stay out of the weeds as we angled downward.

We raised a ruckus that the Thompson Hounds heard every decibel of. They were going nuts, and the next flight of steps was in front of their domain. We dashed past them, positioned the ladder on the steps, and click-clacked the rest of the way to the bottom. Once down, we figured out an even faster way to slide down the steps. We placed the ladder over the top of the railings, and we grabbed a rung and kicked off. We scraped down over the tops of the railings laughing until our bellies ached from just too much fun. Finally, we decided to stash our ladder/go-cart back under the steps for another day and we each headed home.

My mother was a great cook, and no matter what we were having for dinner, it would be good, except for the things I refused to eat. We grew up eating what was put on the table and were rarely given the right of refusal. However, my dad didn't eat liver or chitlins, and I fell right in behind him with a distaste for and a refusal to eat them. We were fortunate enough to have apple, peach, cherry, and pear trees in our yard, and berries on vines in our garden. It was not uncommon for homes in our hillside community to have large yards or extensive tracts of land. So, with the availability of all of that fruit, it was no wonder that pies and cobblers were commonplace on our dinner table. My mother canned pears, and in the winter months, hot pear preserves over homemade biscuits kick-started many a cold and frosty day.

Although there was no set time for dinner, we all seemed to show up at about the same time every day. It was vibrational, spiritual if you will, but the day's essence seemed to center around dinner. It was our time to connect as a family unit, and exceptions were rare. We were a close-knit family and other than the time that my mother and father worked, they were generally home and provided a stable home environment. My dad played pinochle once a month at a friend's house and often spent Saturday afternoons at the pool hall but we all knew where he was. We never saw or heard our parents argue. We knew that they had to have had disagreements, but they reserved them for private times and presented a united front to us and were particularly of one mind when it came to us children.

At times, that "one mind" made decisions that were fundamentally sound and full of ethical guidelines, but difficult for me to understand or accept as wise or fair. I can't forget what happened one day after a fight with my sisters. They used to gang up on me and beat me up and lock me in the closet until it was close to the time my parents were due back home. This went on until, one day, they had locked me in the closet and, unbeknownst to them, my cousin Butch had shown me how to get out of the closet with a hanger. I had stashed several hangers inside and then, finding one in the dark, used it to make my escape.

I climbed the steps to the second floor only to find my sisters sitting on my bed laughing about having beaten me up. I became infuriated and walked over to my oldest sister and punched her in the mouth. I put my fists up and threatened both of them with more of the same. To my surprise, they backed away to the wall behind the bed while tears streamed down Janet's face. It was a liberating moment for me and signaled the end of their ability to beat me up.

When my parents learned what had transpired, my father took me aside and spanked me for punching my sister in the mouth and lectured me on the reasons why men shouldn't hit women. I was livid to say the least. They had jumped me and I had successfully retaliated, and I couldn't fathom why I was the only one being punished. However, that was not only the last time I would hit either of my sisters; it became the last time that I would ever hit any woman. That lesson I learned from my father segued into the dominant culture of the neighborhood and the crew of guys I would eventually hang out with. In our group you were considered less than a man if you were a woman beater.

Anyway, I soon discovered that there were far better ways to torture one's sisters without laying a hand on them. My favorite thing to do when only the three of us were home was to go into the bathroom, lock the door, crawl out of the second-story window, hang from the window sill, and jump down to the concrete below. I would run off and play for hours while my sisters were at home pounding on the bathroom door to no avail. Later, I would get my dad's ladder, lean it on the side of the house and climb up and in through the window. When I exited the bathroom, my sisters were mad enough to strangle me because they had to go to a neighbor's house to use their bathroom.

After dinner, my mother insisted that I bathe and get ready for bed because we would be up early getting ready for Sunday school. It was either Sunday school or church and sometimes both. For the children, Sunday school was preferred because church services were long and hot in our small, stuffy church that, of course, had no air conditioning.

Sunday came and left uneventfully, and soon it was Monday morning and time for school. There were only two weeks before summer vacation, and I was attending Baxter, which was the third elementary school for me. Before Baxter, I went to Crescent, which was to say the least, interesting and trying. There, I encountered a strange and cruel teacher, hated and feared by all of her students. She was a strict disciplinarian who had a prosthetic hand over which she wore a tight black leather glove. We all swore that it was metal because that's what it felt like, and most of us experienced what it felt like. Her particular brand of discipline was harsh; she would make us bend our heads down over our desks as she pounded on our backs with her prosthetic hand. It was a frightening experience for the uninitiated.

We took every opportunity to get back at her though, like putting tacks on her chair, glue on her papers, or spitting in her coffee and stirring it with a pencil. It was primary school warfare, and we were all combatants. The only way we won, however, was to transfer out of her classroom and out of Crescent. So Baxter was a win-win situation for me because it was closer to home and thus a shorter and safer walk for me.

My mother worked at Pittsburgh Hospital and would often walk with me to school on her way to work. She would kiss me on the cheek at our departure point, and I would cross the street to school. When I got to my homeroom and sat at my desk, Jeanie Harriston and Cookie Sloan often reminded me that I had lipstick on my cheek and would wipe it off for me.

They were my first real girl friends, not in the romantic sense but in the true sense of the word friend. I credit them with helping me to understand that not only could women be great friends but that having women friends was a necessary part of life. Often, I talked with each of them on the telephone after school or visited them at their homes. I didn't understand the feelings that I had for them then but somehow I felt as though they were fundamental, that daily contact with them was essential. My experiences with them, combined with the relationship I eventually formed with my sisters and the observation of my father's gentle way with my mother, helped me to develop an ability to communicate with women and display a particular sensitivity to them.

Two weeks passed quickly, and summer vacation was a welcome reality. One of my best friends, Lawrence Rembert, came back to Pittsburgh for several months. He spent the winter months in Cleveland with his father and the summer months in Pittsburgh with his mother. He, Art Davis, who was another best friend, and I were like the three musketeers as we fished and swam and hung out during the summer months. This summer, however, was not without its tribulations. One Saturday afternoon, my cousin Kathy and I were walking up Brushton Avenue and were about a half block from my house. We were passing the home of one of the few white people still living in the community when her door opened suddenly and the woman who lived there grabbed me by the arm and pulled me inside. She locked her door and stood in front of it refusing to let me leave. Kathy banged and kicked on the door and then dashed off to get help.

While Kathy was going for help, this gibbering woman with fiery red hair began to interrogate me about her garbage cans. Apparently, someone had been repeatedly setting them on fire, and she was convinced I knew something about it.

I was clueless about her garbage cans and agitated over her inquisition. She was holding onto my arm and intensely questioning me. I yanked away from her grip and told her that she had better move away from the door. Then I caught a glimpse through her kitchen window at an ensuing drama that would be sure to frighten her to death. It was my mother, looking like the warrior queen of a neighborhood tribe on a mission to rescue one of her babies. She was coming down the steps in front of our house with my Aunt Velma, my sisters, and three of my cousins behind her. My mother had been straightening her hair and it was sticking straight up and out in all directions, which added at least a foot to her height, and was clutching the straightening comb in her hand in a menacing fashion. Seeing this, I immediately turned to my red-headed captor and said, "Aw man, my mama's gonna kill you." She ran to her window to see what I was talking about, and when she turned back around, she was as pale as an individual could be and still be alive. It looked as though all of the blood in her body had rushed to her hair. She reached for the telephone to call the police as I ran back to the window and saw that the number of people behind my mother had grown to a small crowd. By the time my mother had reached the door, the whole neighborhood had coalesced behind her and was soon at every window and door of the house.

My mother banged on the door and yelled, "Open up this door right now." The woman opened the door with the chain on it, but my mother and aunt banged and pushed on the door until the chain popped off and the door swung open. My mother grabbed me and pushed me outside and, pointing her finger, exclaimed, " If you ever touch another child of mine I'll snatch you-bald headed."

"And I'll snatch any hair she misses," my aunt added. The rest of the neighborhood chimed in, and it was becoming an ugly scene by the time that the police arrived. The first officer out of the squad car tried to calm everyone down in order to find out what had happened. My family was livid, insisting that this woman was in trouble and that they needed to straighten her out. The police had positioned themselves between what seemed like all of Homewood and this one little white woman with paint-red hair. It took at least a half of an hour to sort out what happened and calm everyone down. The police admonished the woman who had grabbed me and asked my mother if she would accept her apology or if she wanted to press charges. My mother wanted neither and reiterated her warning as she motioned for us to leave. Slowly, the crowd dissipated and returned to what they were doing before this all had happened.

Of course, I was innocent. I neither knew who had been setting those garbage cans on fire nor that it had even been happening. I didn't have to convince my parents that I was innocent. They knew that I wasn't capable of or foolish enough to do something like that. My father was particularly upset when he heard about the day's events and told me to walk on the other side of the street away from Crazy Red's (as we began to call her) house. I didn't have to do that for long because, a month later, the house with the burning garbage cans and its fiery-red-haired occupant was vacant and up for sale.

With that as an introduction to summer, the following two and a half months were anticlimactic except for the time that my cousin Ollie dived out of the front seat of a moving cab. One afternoon he, my mother, and his baby brother Bobby were coming home from the hospital as he reached for the knob to roll down the window but grabbed the door knob instead. The door swung open as the cab turned the corner, and he rolled out onto the sidewalk. Bobby raised up in the back seat and pointed outside as if to say, "there he goes." Ollie was okay, but for the rest of the summer at least, he avoided opening windows in moving cars, and diving out onto cement sidewalks.

Swimming, fishing, rock throwing, hide-and-seek and a few fist fights rounded out the rest of my summer vacation, and I was soon trudging back and forth to Baxter for my last year of grade school. Then, one fall afternoon, a couple of my buddies suggested we go down to Westinghouse High School to watch the varsity football game. Westinghouse was famous, even legendary in Pittsburgh and Western Pennsylvania. They had an extraordinary record of winning city championships. Opponents couldn't figure out why the team was so successful. There was something special, unique, even mysterious about this dominant team smack dab in the middle of the black community. They were a tremendous source of pride and dignity for Homewood, and school spirit revolved around them. Its players enjoyed celebrity status in the community and throughout the city. Yet, as I learned later, there was an obvious paradox. For despite this team's dominant, successful, legendary stature, there were few or no scholarship opportunities for its players. There were very few college recruiters knocking on the doors of Westinghouse, and a pitiful number of players received scholarships.

Nonetheless, we were on our way to the school to watch the game. We had to run all the way in order to make it there before kick-off. We made excellent time and even made it there before the team came out of the locker room. We climbed over an outside fence and squeezed under a small opening, just the right size for sixth graders to fit through. We ran to the top of the hill overlooking the field and the bleachers. The opposing team was already on the field, and the band and students filled every available seat with hundreds of people standing, waiting for an afternoon of fun and excitement.

Suddenly, the Westinghouse locker room erupted in loud boisterous noise, drawing the attention of everyone in earshot. The door burst open and the team, yelling at the top of their lungs, roared onto the upper deck, headed straight toward where I was standing. As the bright afternoon sun contrasted the blue and gold uniforms against the gray and black background of the school, I stood like a deer in front of car headlights, awestruck; I couldn't move. The team charged toward the fence and me, and all I could manage to do was to sit down and cover my head with my hands. Soon they were leaping over the fence, and I was crouched down looking up through my folded hands at this thunderous throng of blue and gold humanity soaring over me. This was too surreal. I flashed back to the sidewalk in front of Ruby's store and the dreams I had that night. What was this blue and gold thing that had come into my life and seemed to position itself over me and in close proximity to pain and danger?

When the dust cleared and the squad was headed down the hill, one blue and gold behemoth stood over me. He was huge. It seemed as though he was eight feet tall and, in shoulder pads and a helmet, was the biggest living thing I had ever encountered in all of my eleven years on the planet. He looked down at me and in a deep bass voice that seemed to come from under the grass on which I was sitting said, "Hey little man you're still alive ain't you?" Suffice it to say, I was speechless. He reached down, picked me up, lifted me over the fence and said, "Come on with me." We walked down the hill together, and when we got to the front row of the bleachers he stopped. With one hand he pushed several people further down the row and cleared a spot.

"Sit here," he said and walked onto the field.

"Thanks," I replied, finally managing to find the voice to speak. "Man," I thought, "this is really cool." It was the first time I had ever been that close to a real football game and I had been ushered there by a giant. The game was exciting and Westinghouse punished its opponent by some ridiculous score, and when it was over, I climbed the steps to the upper field and found my friends standing at the fence. They ran over to me, exclaiming how lucky I had been and how they wished they could have sat where I did to watch the game. "Not if you almost got stomped by the whole team," I said.

As we walked home, I couldn't help but think about the scary and exciting events of the afternoon and whether my next encounter with that strange blue and gold phenomena would leave me dead or alive, or both.

CHAPTER 3

"In the Circle in The Room"

My interest had been piqued about Westinghouse High School, and I wanted to know more about the football team. I was completing my last year at Baxter and would be starting at Westinghouse in the fall, where seventh through twelfth graders attended school together. Although junior and senior high classes were held in separate parts of the building there were no barriers, physical or other, between the two, but the differences were, of course, obvious. Going to school with so many people and in such a large building would be challenging, but I was becoming more excited at the prospects each day. Every chance I got, I ran to Westinghouse with my friends for the home games and was never disappointed at the spectacle on the field. Westinghouse had a prime time band that enjoyed a stellar reputation of its own, and majorettes and cheerleaders added to the exhibition on the field. The team won every game I watched and continued to dominate city sports.

I got through sixth grade, graduated and then experienced an unexpected vacation far away from home. During the early part of June, my uncle J.C. from Louisiana visited us and persuaded my parents to allow me to return to Lake Charles, Louisiana, with him. My mother was born and raised in Lake Charles, and still had relatives and friends living there. The trip and my stay in the South turned out to be truly an eye-opener for me. Although Pittsburgh was no bastion of egalitarianism, I had my first real experience with blatant, overt racism and discrimination during this visit. My uncle and I traveled by bus to Lake Charles, and he warned me about southern traditions and restrictions. As soon as we passed the Mason-Dixon Line, I was formally introduced to Jim Crow. We were relegated to the back of the bus and could eat only at the "Colored Sections" in the terminal, which were poorly appointed and maintained. We could only use the "Colored Bathrooms" which were usually dirty and rarely equipped with supplies. The attitudes were noticeably different. We were treated with disdain, like excess baggage accompanying first-class white passengers. I took these affronts personally and was reluctant to comply with the restrictions. My uncle had to restrain me from sitting in the white part of the restaurants and would not let me go anywhere in the terminals alone. I was truly what they referred to in the South as uppity, and found it hard to understand why my relatives would continue to live there.

It was a huge adjustment for me to go from the covert discrimination of Northern city life to the kind of social system that could bring physical harm and even death for noncompliance. On Saturdays in Lake Charles, my oldest cousin J.C. Jr. and I were allowed to take the city bus into town for a few hours. On one of those excursions, I took a drink from a "Whites Only," fountain and it took my cousin's youthful but considerable Southern social skills to keep us from physical harm. I was just not used to looking for a sign over a public fountain before drinking. Other than those issues, however, I had a ball in Louisiana, and before I knew it the time had come to return home to Pittsburgh. My aunt and uncle sat me down and seriously discussed the importance of compliance with Southern traditions on my trip home. I would be travelling alone, and it was a three-day voyage. They gave me a large bag of food they had prepared. They figured that by the time I needed to buy food, I would have crossed the Mason-Dixon Line and would have been allowed to eat anywhere I wanted to in the terminals. My aunt and uncle instructed me to use the bathroom on the bus in order to avoid issues with restricted public restrooms.

 So, my journey back home began with a sendoff in Downtown Lake Charles. The three- day trip would be more than a notion for a twelve-year-old travelling alone, simply due to the number of bus transfers and connections to be made. I kept to myself on the bus and didn't engage in idle conversation with any of the other passengers. When the bus stopped for short intervals at non-transfer points, I would get off to stretch my legs but never wandered more than a few feet from the bus. I made it home without issue, and breathed a sigh of relief at the sight of my father waiting to meet me at the terminal in Pittsburgh. It felt good to be home and, I was proud of the fact that I had traveled all that distance by myself without missing a single connection. I had about a week of summer vacation left before I would begin my first day as a seventh grader at Westinghouse and lost no time reacquainting myself with home, family, and friends.

My first day at Westinghouse came quickly enough, and like most seventh graders I was overwhelmed at the size of the school, the number of students and the level of noise in the hallways between classes. As the days and weeks passed, I became acclimated to my new environment. I began to notice football players in the hallways and perceived something different about them. They all seemed to have an air of confidence, a machismo, and a seriousness that was lacking in other students. They all hung together, enjoying extraordinary camaraderie, and they appeared to have the respect of the entire student body. Physically fit, they swaggered down the hallways, but were never obnoxious or arrogant. There was always a vein of restraint, however, some controlling element to which they all answered, something beneath the surface that was sinister and intimidating. It was something that communicated a oneness, a purpose, maybe even a raison d'ettre. On football game days, the team all wore blue and gold jerseys with a bulldog design in the upper left corner. They carried themselves in a reverent manner as though they were preparing for battle. They were all serious, very serious about what each and every one of them was expected to do.

I had no idea how steeped in tradition the team was, but my curiosity was growing stronger with each passing day. I knew of the old expression "curiosity killed the cat," but I also understood that "satisfaction brought it back." I was becoming more and more interested in ferreting out the truth behind the mysteries and myths. I began to suspect there was a deep, secretive part of this story of success and legend, and I sensed I would come to experience it all firsthand.

I spent my seventh and eighth grade years largely as a spectator to the whole high school scene, and during the summer before I was to enter ninth grade I decided to try out for the junior varsity football team. I had been asking questions about the football program and had heard like most people in Homewood about "The Room." "The Room" referred to the locker room where football players got dressed for games, exercise, and practice and was the place where team meetings were held. Whenever I mentioned to anyone that I was going to try out for the football team, the response I usually got was "Are you crazy?" That was generally followed by, "You don't want to be in The Room, man." The operative expression appeared to be, "Many are called, but few are foolish enough to answer."

I came to understand that the weeding-out process was not only difficult physically but emotionally as well. It all began by trying out for the junior varsity squad. That meant that, as an initiate, I would enter the organization as what was known as a "scrub scrub," which was a lowly nonentity who was junior to a "scrub." Scrubs, of course, were tenth graders who had been through the entry program as a junior varsity player. I would spend several months in the junior varsity program until graduating to the more serious initiation in "The Room." The term scrub originally came from the fact that initiates to the football program were forced to take home the dirty gym clothes of old guys, (those who had successfully completed the initiation phase as a scrub and had been granted full membership status), wash them, and bring them back the next day.

The entrée to all of this came during August, and it required attending an early morning meeting in The Room, after which an exercise and practice session was to follow. Fortunately, Art Davis, who was an old guy by then, had schooled me on the rules and traditions of The Room. The most serious of which was recognition of and respect for "The Circle."

The Circle was imaginary and existed in the middle of the pyramid-shaped locker room. The base of the pyramid was the wall immediately to the right as one entered The Room. The sides angled toward the back and culminated in what was referred to as the lettermen's section. This section was reserved for those players who had earned a varsity letter. Art had warned me to never walk through the middle of The Circle. That was reserved for old guys. Newcomers were admonished never to encroach upon the interior of The Circle. The only person who could grant temporary permission for a scrub to enter The Circle was the team leader. Punishment for encroachment was severe. There was, however, benevolence in the administration of punishment. The perpetrator was allowed to select the method of punishment. It could either be taking the towels or The Circle. Taking the towels meant dropping your pants and shorts and taking fifty-two strokes with a towel that had been wet at the tip and pulled through a knot. The towel was wielded with brutal force and left the rule breaker severely bruised and bleeding. Taking The Circle meant fighting the leader of the team. If one chose to fight the leader of the team and won, no further punishment would be administered. Of course, the tradition in The Room meant that there was no such thing as a fair fight between an old guy and anyone else in the world. Therefore, fighting the leader meant taking on the entire team at once.

With this knowledge uppermost in my mind, I headed toward The Room for my first day as an initiate in this cult of football worship. When I got to the door, my heart was beating so fast that it felt like one continuous beat. I followed in behind two other guys and looked for an open spot on the benches reserved for newcomers. After walking down three short concrete steps, I saw the only open space available and began toward it along what I perceived to be the outer perimeter of The Circle. I was uncertain of the proper boundaries and was tentative on my approach. I couldn't help but wonder whether I had stepped on or over the border, or what would happen if I tripped over someone's feet and fell into The Circle. I wondered if that would be seen as an accident or whether I would be guilty of violating the sacred code and subject to discipline. In my mind, I questioned why they just hadn't outlined it with paint and thought that it would have been easier for everybody involved.

There would be no uncertainty then, and it should be obvious to the most casual of observers that it was there for a purpose. However, the fact that it was only seeable by the mind's eye and was fundamental to the cult's tradition and daily rituals made it a much more powerful reality. It was an invisible, immovable object, backed by irresistible forces and all were duty bound to observe and protect it. There was only one exception to the rule and that was made for the coach. No outsiders were ever allowed in The Room.

I made my way to the empty spot on the bench and sat down next to my fellow initiates. There was no conversation amongst us, just blank stares as we were careful not to make eye contact with anyone. Soon, the leader, Charlie, walked to the door and locked it. No sooner had the lock clicked than there was a knock on the door. It was another guy who said, "I'm here to try out." Charlie let him in and told him to take a seat. He walked down the steps, straight through the middle of The Circle, walked to where I was sitting, and squeezed in next to me. A lump the size of a medium toad jumped to the middle of my throat as I wondered why this guy had to have chosen to sit next to me. I scrunched my shoulders together in an attempt to make myself smaller and less noticeable, but I was being illuminated by his irreverent glow. Everyone looked at him in disbelief and before anyone could respond, the coach walked into the room and began the meeting.

After the coach explained what would be happening on the field for the next few hours, he left and Charlie locked the door behind him. The silence was deafening. As Charlie walked to the middle of The Circle, a visibly throbbing vein on the side of his forehead grew with each step he took. He turned in my direction, frowned, and gritted his teeth. I was afraid of guilt by association or at least by proximity as Charlie asked, "What's your name?" By that time, I had forgotten my name and had become a motionless, frozen piece of bug-eyed flesh and bones sitting on a splintered bench on an unknown planet somewhere in a far-off galaxy. "Dub," came the reply from my immediate left, and to say that I was relieved would be textbook understatement.

"Dub, hunh," Charlie replied. "Dub, you walked through The Circle, you're gonna have to take the towels or fight me."

"What circle? I don't see no circle," Dub replied. It was clear that he was clueless about the tradition in The Room and especially about The Imaginary Circle. He was physically fit and had skills a number of people in the community had recognized. Someone had convinced him to try out for the team, but why he hadn't been schooled about protocol is anybody's guess. Gifted athletes were a definite asset to the team, but cult-like obedience to the way of The Room and reverence for The Imaginary Circle took precedence over talent and ability.

Dub was in for a rude awakening, probably one of the scariest moments of his young life. Charlie walked to the back of the lettermen's section, picked up a towel and pulled it into a knot on one end. He walked into the shower, wet the tip of the towel and walked back to the middle of The Circle.

"Come here, man," he said, motioning to Dub. Dub got up and walked straight through the middle of The Circle again. Charlie snapped the towel a couple of times testing its readiness.

"Drop your pants. You're gonna take the towels," Charlie told Dub.

"I ain't takin nothin'," Dub replied, and started walking toward the door. Charlie grabbed his arm and pulled him back into the middle of The Circle. Then Charlie dropped the towel and swung a right hook towards Dub's face. Dub had a little reputation in the community for fighting and was known to be able to handle himself in a boxing match. He ducked under Charlie's right hook and reached for his legs in an attempt to jack him up and slam him to the floor. The "jack," as it was known, was rudimentary fight repertoire for every African American male in Pittsburgh.

We learned how to administer it an early age, as well as how to defend against it. The basic procedure was to duck down under an opponent's punch, grab his legs and lift him off the ground. Then you would attempt to body slam him to the ground, or onto a parked car, or any stationary object in close proximity. Stomping the guy with one's feet until victory could be declared usually followed.

As soon as Dub reached for Charlie's legs, the benches where the old guys were sitting cleared and the scene resembled the running of the bulls in Pamplona Spain.

It was sheer pandemonium, and Dub disappeared under too many fists and feet to count. He must have had a direct line of communication open to God that day because miraculously he emerged on the other side of the pile reaching for the locked door. It was almost comical because everyone except us spectators still thought he was under the pile. He pulled himself up the steps by his hands, reached the door, and, unlocking it, fled down the hallway. Several gave chase but soon returned panting and expressing disbelief at Dub's speed and agility. His exit was permanent, and as long as he did not return to The Room no one would bother him. Undoubtedly, his athleticism would have benefited the team. There were a lot of guys who were either beaten or frightened out of The Room or who were discouraged due to the strictly enforced adherence to the code.

Charlie stood at the door holding it wide open offering a last chance for the faint of heart to escape without harm. No one moved. I sat tight partly because I did not trust the offer of safe passage and remained against my better judgement. The grueling exercise and practice that followed were worse than what I imagined. Extremely difficult workouts and tough scrimmages were part and parcel of the conditioning program even for those of us involved in the junior varsity program. After that intro, those of us playing junior varsity football would not visit The Room again until the second half of the year. We were scrub scrubs and junior to the scrubs who were being initiated all year in The Room, and who were subject to the full extent of varsity terrorism. They would take out their frustrations on us after having been pummeled in The Room.

Scrub scrubs were the laughingstock of the day when arriving on the field to play a football game. We were given, rather we searched for football gear in old drums in the JV locker room. We wore vintage helmets with no face guards or chinstraps, helmets that could not have protected us from a good smack by someone's bare hand. They could be folded and tucked under an armpit. The football cleats we wore had so many spikes missing from them that we often wobbled walking or running up and down the field. The jerseys and pants we wore were no better. But no one was forced to stay. In fact, the converse was true. Everything that was done was designed to make us quit or make us tougher than we ever dreamed we could be.

CHAPTER 4

"Cult Tradition"

Had we had enough or would we opt to become human punching bags for old guys in the varsity program? With the month of December came the end of the junior varsity season and decision-making time. Continuing on meant graduating to scrub status and entering training for the next season in January in The Room. Scrubs who had lorded over us in the junior varsity program had become old guys and would be eager to exercise their newly acquired powers over a fresh crop of initiates. The videotape of my first trip to The Room played over and over in my head as I debated a normal existence versus an entire year of fear, intimidation, extortion, and physical abuse. Naturally, I opted for the latter, as did half of the junior varsity team. There was a strong contingent of us going over to the varsity program that lived within a several block radius of each other. We had begun to form a little clique of support and commiseration that would pull us through the tough times ahead.

We were a motley crew of young boys with varying degrees of athletic ability and talent. There were, of course, two old guys from our little neighborhood who had preceded us in The Room. They were George Webb, a talented fullback, who lived on Monticello Street, and Art Davis, who, of course, was one of my closest friends. Art lived up the hill from me and had gained a bit of a reputation in The Room when he was a scrub. He and another scrub named Burgess would often laugh when being beaten which angered their transgressors, who increased the intensity of the beating as Art and his cohort continued to laugh. Burgess dropped from the program for some reason but Art continued, and in his senior year played first string guard. Lawrence Rembert lived two doors from me and joined the team in the summer when he returned from Cleveland. He was strong, physically fit and a little more mature than most guys his age were. Dave Young lived across the street from Art and joined us in the late spring.

Young would grow to become an integral part of our group and play a key role in one of the more serious dramas we would face in our tenure as scrubs. He was known as the best street fighter in the city of Pittsburgh and, although his reputation preceded him, his persona led one to believe that it couldn't have belonged to him. He was unassuming, fair-minded and good-natured. We never knew him to start a fight, and in fact, he was often the peacemaker. He was so self-confident that he could walk away from a challenge, but his situation was like it was in the Wild West with gun fighters. Everybody wanted to challenge the guy with the reputation for being the fastest gun. When all else failed though, Young had no equal in a street fight.

Quick with his hands, he was known to circle to the left of his opponent, body punching him in the side from the shoulders to his knees, weakening and softening up that side of his body. Then a sharp punch behind the knee would drop Young's opponent a foot or two, setting him up for a powerful straight left jab. Then with Young's execution of the jack with lightning speed and precision, it was all over but the shoutin'. Young had also been known to hang out with a couple of guys who had reputations of their own. Two of them were known as Horse Jerry and Knuckles. Horse Jerry earned his reputation when he punched a huge farm horse in the head and knocked it out. Knuckles earned his by punching a guy in the forehead and leaving the imprint of his knuckles in the in the guy's unconscious skull. The fact that Young was one of our friends bolstered our reputation in the streets as well.

Albert Bridges and Clifford Walker lived next door to each other and a block away from me on Pineridge Street. Bridges, a jazz aficionado, as we all were, was slight of build and an unlikely candidate for the rigors of Westinghouse's football program but would prove to be stalwart and tenacious. Walker, more physically fit, had a robust sense of humor and an up-tempo outlook on life. Malcolm Jones lived a half of a block from Walker and Bridges on Hermitage Street, was of average height and build, but was athletically capable. Joe Avent lived a block and a half from me on Monticello Street. He was the shortest member of our crew and had the speed and inclination of a running back. Leo Loar lived a half of a block from Joe on Monticello Street and was the most gifted athlete among us. Tall and a ferocious competitor, he excelled in football, track, and basketball. Michael Peeler, Iron Mike, as we called him, lived several blocks away from Leo on Frankstowne Avenue. Peeler was physically strong with an ever present chip on his shoulder and an in your face kind of style and attitude. Then, I rounded out the crew: Frank Reed, or Reed as I was called. I was of slightly less than average build with slightly less than average football skills.

As January approached, we gathered to talk about what was going to happen in The Room, and how, if at all possible, we could prepare for the awesome eventuality. We met at Leo's house, which would soon become the gathering spot for our crew for our entire tour of duty. We shared rumors and stories about The Room, and the seven of us, Leo, Joe, Walker, Peeler, Bridges, Malcolm, and I, vowed to make it through together.

The dreaded day to enter the varsity program came too soon. The way the football program worked would have us participating from January through November, concluding after the city high school championship game. The team had become so used to winning that the football program was wrapped around the championship game. Returning players and hopefuls all shared the seventh period of the day together. It was the last class period of the school day, and it allowed for exercise, practice, and other facets of the program to be experienced as a unit.

The bell rang signaling the end of the sixth period, and I thought about not going to The Room and just enjoying the rest of the day, but I ran into Peeler, Joe, and Walker in the hallway, and their momentum carried me along with them. Leo, Malcolm, and Bridges joined us on the stairway leading to the archway preceding the football and basketball locker rooms. We were somewhat emboldened by a sense of togetherness and completed our journey to The Room door without hesitancy. It was open and several guys were already seated in the scrub section to the right of the steps. We walked in and took the immediately available seats on an open bench.

"More fresh meat," someone yelled from the back and several pairs of tennis shoes came flying out of nowhere toward our bench. Instinctively, we all ducked under the airborne soles.

"What are you punks duckin' for, you afraid of a tennis shoe?" yelled a voice from the back of the lettermen's section.

"You better not duck again," someone else said as more shoes soared in our direction. We all sat still and, fortunately, all of the tennis shoes missed their mark.

"Aw, now y'all got heart, hunh? We'll see how much heart you got," exclaimed yet another voice.

Soon the benches in the scrub section were full of hopefuls, and Charlie Harris, the team captain and leader walked to the door, pulled it shut with a bang and locked it. Charlie was an exceptional football player. He made the first string varsity squad as a freshman, an extremely rare accomplishment. He not only had the allegiance of the team, but also commanded the respect of the entire squad. He spoke in a compelling voice, and his words were autocratic. He epitomized the rough-hewn image of the captain of a brutish squad of football thugs. He had earned the role of captain, and no one ever questioned his authority or his ability and no one dared question the exalted status of The Imaginary Circle. But Charlie also had charisma and a larger-than-life personality that made him perfect for the job as captain.

Cult Of The Imaginary Circle

The protocols of the cult were law, handed down from preceding squads of iron-willed ancestors, protocols we were about to accept and agree to obey until we ceremoniously exited the brotherhood.

It was so strange, though, to think that a group of young boys (we were all between the ages of fourteen and eighteen) could be so serious about anything, but all one had to do was to look at all of our faces. There were no smiles, only intimidating frowns from the elders of the brotherhood and masked, expressionless stares of huddled inductees.

Charlie walked to the middle of The Circle to hand down the edict. "This is law, y'all," he began and laid out the terms of our existence for the next eleven months. We had to come to The Room every school day for seventh period until our final season in twelfth grade. We were to bring clothes to work out in: a shirt, a pair of shorts, socks, and tennis shoes, and be prepared to stay after school for one-on-one drills or team meetings. We had to be there everyday. If we were sick and didn't come to school, we had better be well by seventh period. We had to ultimately respect The Circle. No one but old guys were allowed to walk within its perimeter. The only exception was the coach. If we were caught walking through The Circle, we would have to take the towels or fight the leader and thus the whole team. If we let someone other than an old guy walk through it, we would suffer the same punishment. We had heard the story of an old guy who was beaten with a bull rope just for letting a couple of guys cut through The Room. It was sacred territory, and no outsiders were ever allowed in. We had to wear khakis and a plain shirt to school everyday. We were warned not to wear anything expensive or even halfway decent because if an old guy wanted it, he would take it. We had a curfew every night until after the championship game in November. We had to be in by 9:00 p.m. or suffer the towels or take on The Circle, and getting caught smoking or drinking carried the same penalties.

We were told we had to do whatever an old guy told us to do unless it was something that we knew was wrong. Then we would just suffer a physical beating for not doing it rather than the consequences of doing something stupid. Lettermen outranked old guys, and the captain outranked everybody except the coach.

We were not allowed into the lettermen's section of the showers and were restricted to the use of one showerhead.

The entire system was designed to weed out those who weren't strong enough or committed enough to the team's reason for existing, which was winning football championships. Rarely were initiates cut from the team. Grueling physical exercise, extensive practice and the scrub cycle were natural eliminators. If hopefuls could hang on until after the championship game was over, they were accepted as permanent members of the team. Although it was rare for anyone to be cut from the team due to lack of skill, maximum effort was absolutely demanded, and poor performance often drew physical punishment.

After the sermon in The Circle and the handing down of the scrub commandments, it was time to get dressed for our first workout with the varsity squad. Most of us could only fold our clothes and lay them down behind the benches. There were only a few hooks on the wall in the scrub section. When we were ready to go, there was just one more small detail that had to be covered. Whenever the team was in transit to the field or the gym and during workouts, practice, and games, it was traditional for scrubs to yell at the tops of their voices. Our traditional chant was "heyyyy now, sayyyyy now," and it was a continuous effort unless silenced by the coach or the captain. It was a siren so to speak, alerting all in close proximity to yield the right of way. We soon discovered, in fact, on the way to the gym, that it also camouflaged the sounds that fists made as we were being punched in transit.

Once in the gym, we began the exercise routine by running twenty laps, filling the gym with our incessant scrub chant. After we finished running laps, we lined up for wind sprints and formed four lanes with an old guy assuming leadership of each lane. It was, of course, a competition, and the pressure was on each of us to win the heat we were in or be seen as responsible for embarrassing an old guy if his lane lost. Waiting to run the next heat, I was approached by an old guy and asked for a Kleenex. I raised my hands and said, "not on me." He wasn't amused and punched me in the chest hard enough to take my breath away. Then he made me turn around and took the back of my shirt and blew his nose on it.

He then became concerned about appearances, as it would look unsightly so he made me tuck my shirt in my shorts. My turn was up next and, fortunately, my competition was three heavyweights and I won my heat. Those who lost suffered at the back of the line.

After several sprints, we circled up to continue the exercise routine. It started with pushups and we followed the lead of one of the old guys known for his stamina and physique. I lost count at fifty pushups and my arms were shaking as I forced my body to comply. We were being watched and anybody who dogged the workout would be punished back in The Room. Sit-ups followed, and leg lifts followed them. Each portion of the workout seemed more difficult than the preceding one, and sweat no longer beaded on my forehead. It rose to the surface in waves and poured over my face, burning my eyes and salting my tongue. Next came the climbing of the ropes suspended from the ceiling and appearing to be ten stories high. Exhausted by then, very few of us made it to the top, a fact that did not go unnoticed, particularly as several fell to the floor when shaking arms gave way. The workout concluded with several finishing laps around the gym, and we headed back, eager to dress and go home. A surprise awaited us when we arrived back in The Room, where we thought we had left our clothes. They had been ransacked and anything of value or in decent condition had been taken, including shoes and socks. Searching for my clothes, I couldn't help but take in the drama unfolding immediately to my right. Two old guys took positions on each side of a scrub. One told him to jump up and the other told him not to. In a state of confusion he just stood there and was immediately knocked over the bench for not jumping up. Struggling to his feet, he was admonished for disrespecting an old guy and was told to jump up. This time he jumped up and upon landing on the floor again was punched in the chest hard enough to knock him over the bench again. As he pulled himself up again the other old guy warned him not to jump up because it was against his principles. This drama went on like a broken record while other scrubs were being beaten for dogging exercises. Suddenly, a voice from the back of the lettermen's section ordered us out of The Room.

"You scrubs got ten seconds to get out, one, five, nine, ten." Then huge metal football hangers weighing eight to ten pounds were hurled at us while we frantically tried to finish dressing and gather what was left of our pilfered possessions. In order to get out, we had to run through a gauntlet of fists and warnings daring us to return.

Partially dressed and exhausted, our neighborhood crew agreed to meet on the corner after retrieving our coats from school lockers. The seven of us walked home together questioning our sanity and our vow to make it through this ordeal together. It was a definite uncertainty whether anyone would show up the next day.

CHAPTER 5

"Scrub Life"

I wasn't very talkative during dinner and the fact that my older sister, Janet was away at school focused more attention on Ann and me. My parents noticed my quiet, pensive mood and asked if I were feeling okay. Ann, however, had an intuition that it had something to do with my involvement in Westinghouse's football program. I attributed my mood to physical exhaustion and remarked that the exercise program was tougher than I thought it would be. The code of silence was absolute even though we were never told not to talk to anyone about what we were going through as scrubs. If our parents had ever learned of the details, they would surely have made us quit, or worse, may have gone to school officials with complaints. After dinner, I showered and fell into bed without so much as a glance at the books I had brought home. Homework never crossed my mind as my body was in control and signaled an urgent need to recharge its batteries.

The next morning sneaked up on me and would have passed unnoticed but for my mother's voice urging me to get up and get ready for school. I couldn't believe it was morning already because it felt like I had just closed my eyes for a brief moment or two. They were the only parts of my body I could move without pain. I was feeling like I had slept on a mattress stuffed with rocks and sticks and other hurtful things.

Dressed and finally out of the house, I caught up with Walker and Bridges at the corner of Pineridge and Hermitage Streets. We looked like we belonged at the back of a surplus government cheese line. Altogether, we weren't wearing a single thing that an old guy could have been interested in taking. That was all well and good, but our days of looking cool had been put on hold. Our expression for being extremely well dressed was "clean as the board of health," but for a while at least, making an impression with how clean we could get had become a thing of the past. When we got to Collier Street, we saw Joe and Leo standing on the corner of Monticello and Collier and headed their way. They weren't dressed any better than we were, and when we passed Leo's house his sister, Estella, took one look at all of us and burst into laughter.

"Don't y'all think you're overdoin' it a bit?" she asked in between uncontrollable giggles. We really didn't care what we looked like as long as we returned home wearing what we had left with.

It was evident to us as we walked the halls at school that there had been some attrition from our initial group of thirty scrubs. Obviously any scrub dressed in good clothes had no intention of continuing, but our crew of seven had all decided to proceed, still vowing not to punk out.

Lunch that day was a reality that forced us to develop coping strategies for the rest of the year. We should have known that guys who had taken our shoes and socks the day before were capable of taking our lunch the next day as though it were a sacrosanct privilege. We just hadn't focused on lunch as something to be concerned about. We knew we needed to eat in order to have energy enough to make it through strenuous exercises during seventh-period workouts. Joe, Bridges, and I were in line together in the cafeteria and, after paying for our food, we looked for someplace to sit. Two old guys sitting at a table in the back of the cafeteria signaled for us to join them. We walked over to where they were sitting, put our trays on the table and sat down. Then, much to our chagrin, they took the food off of our trays and proceeded to eat it as we watched. We weren't the only ones deprived of sustenance that day. Stories abounded of hungry scrubs watching their lunches being scarfed down by varsity squad gluttons. After that day, the lunchroom became off limits for us as we took to hiding in inconspicuous places and getting friends and relatives to sneak food to us.

Seventh period came quickly, too quickly, as it always did. The days seemed to go by so fast until seventh period arrived and then time dragged on forever. Workouts were still tough and physical, and we remained punching bags and suffered various abuses that depleted our numbers. Three scrubs were caught out after nine-o-clock and took the towels as punishment. They survived the ordeal, but the towels did serious damage.

They had difficulty sitting in class and, for several days, bloodstains could be seen on the backs of their pants. They all quit the team a week later and school a week after that.

They had gained the respect of the whole team, scrubs and old guys alike, because of the way they stood up under the punishment. Guys usually quit before taking the towels not after and especially not after taking the towels like iron men, no tears, no whimpers, no complaints. We never found out why they quit the team or school but they could have been of benefit to the team, and the team could have benefited them. Had they been playing ball, they would most likely have completed high school because the graduation rate for football players was almost a hundred percent.

But scrub life marched on, and then came the phenomenon known as hitting on the mats. After what had seemed like an extraordinarily strenuous workout, we were getting dressed to go home when the door was shut and locked. My heart speed shifted into third gear because that usually signaled something bad was about to transpire. Soon, two old guys emerged from the back of the lettermen's section with a floor mat that they had borrowed from the gym and positioned it in the middle of The Circle. Charlie walked to the mat and described what was going to take place. What it essentially meant was that we were to become blocking dummies for old guys to practice on.

All of this would take place on the mat over the concrete floor without helmets, pads, or any protection other than our jockey straps. Each of us would have the opportunity to test our strength, to show how hard we could hit and how hard of a hit we could absorb without flinching or grimacing. Performance, of course, was demanded. We were expected to hit as hard as we could when instructed to and not to hit, to function as a blocking dummy when instructed to.

The most interesting aspect of all of this was the fact that the mat had been placed in the middle of The Circle. We were so aware and reverent of The Circle that we couldn't understand why this blocking drill couldn't take place in the gym. The Circle had become so real to us that we no longer had to imagine it. It was as much a part of physical reality as the cold hard floor it covered. We developed a sixth sense about it and it became second nature for us to circumnavigate it. When old guys asked for volunteers from among our group, we looked like a canvas painting of fear in still life. Even when it was announced that we could hit on the mats in The Circle without fear of reprisal, no one moved. After reiterating the promise of safe passage, they selected one of us and the drill began, the object of which was for two guys to lunge at each other from a three-point stance and either drive the opponent off of the mat or knock him down. When it was my turn on the mat, I was paired with an old guy who was about thirty pounds heavier and about three inches taller than I was. I had nervously stepped into The Circle and assumed the position. The signal was called and, a second later, I hit the mat with a thunderous thud.

"Reed, you better hit," exclaimed an unidentified voice as I picked myself up from the mat. The next round began when our bodies met forcefully over the center of the mat and I was again knocked off my feet. After several more punishing hits, I was allowed to retreat to the benches and watch the final drills and, soon thereafter, our crew of seven walked gingerly home, tired, sore, and hungry enough to eat a small water buffalo.

As the days rolled by, the number of scrubs remaining in the program dropped from thirty to around twenty, but our crew of seven was still hanging tough. The weather was warming up, and we were soon about to be treated to another experience of scrub life we would never forget. On a warm Friday in April, we were dressed for the seventh-period workout and ready to go to the gym. It was announced, however, that we were going to run to the river and back for our exercise routine that day. The outside door opened, we piped up with our traditional scrub chant and began the trek to the river's edge. We ran down the hill from the locker rooms, across the football field, and up another hill on the other side. We were moving at a pretty fast pace, and keeping up with the pack was, of course, expected without exception. At the top of the hill, we merged into street traffic, dodged a few cars, and ran through a small field of weeds and up onto the railroad tracks. These were active rail lines that freight trains used regularly and they would take us over several trestles and down to the Allegheny River. In the presence of several old guys known for sadistic pranks, I cringed at the thought of being so close to the Allegheny River, deep wide, and notorious for sink-holes and swift currents. I had heard about what happened two years ago when a scrub was forced to hang from a trestle over the river and fell in and almost drowned.

I never knew how far it was to the river's edge but it just felt like too far, especially over railroad tracks and rocks and uneven gravel. There was also the obvious danger of encountering a train while on the tracks, especially since there was very little room on either side and absolutely no room on the trestles. Panting and sweating profusely, we reached the end of the first leg of our journey and paused for a short rest. We had stopped at the foot of a hill next to the far side of the tracks. Before we had a chance to catch our breath, we were told that all of the scrubs had to run to the top of the hill and roll down, and the last one down would be beaten all the way back to the school. It was a hill to be contended with. It slanted on an incline that we could run halfway up, but to get to the top, we had to use both hands and feet. It was full of bricks, weeds, broken glass, thorny bushes, and other debris thrown there by workers clearing the tracks, all of which would be rolled over on our way down.

On the count of three, we charged up the hill, each with serious intention of not being the last one down. I was in a group in the middle of the pack, and as the front runners began their rolling descent downhill, I had to dodge several of them or be knocked down like a duckpin in a bowling alley. Reaching the top, I turned, fell down, and pushed off on a big rock. My descent down was a painful, uncontrolled spin over sharp sticks, rocks, barbed thickets, and pieces of unidentifiable metal. This spectacle was afternoon entertainment for our audience of old guys who sat howling in laughter on the other side of the tracks. Reaching the bottom, I joined the rest of the scrubs who had finished before me and watched the remaining of our compadres hitting rock bottom. My hair was full of dirt and small twigs, and I had several bleeding puncture wounds from objects I had rolled over. My clothes were covered in dirt and thorns and my T-shirt was ripped at the collar. We all looked as though we had been in a ferocious gang fight and had lost miserably.

On the run back to school, we were relieved that there had been no trestle-hanging ordeals to endure, but we agonized over audible thuds and thumps of fists impacting the body of our brother who had been the last scrub down the hill.

Once back in The Room, we hustled to get dressed and out of there, but the coach walked in, took one look at the dried, dead plants and dirt still clinging to our bodies and ordered us all into the showers. That was just what we needed, another hurdle to get over after all that we had endured that day. Scrubs avoided the showers like the plague, especially when the coach was around. There was only one section of the showers we were allowed in, and it had only one showerhead, which dripped water one lousy drop at a time. We knew that, in the past, there had been scrubs ordered back into the showers by the coach when they had emerged dry. So, the shower scene was bizarre to put it mildly. Steaming hot water gushed from six showerheads, which were all empty while one was host to twenty scrubs. The tallest scrubs stretched their hands to the showerhead grabbing the only available drops of moisture while the rest of us were left to scoop water up from the trough before it reached the drain and splash it over our bodies. That allowed us to exit the shower wet and avoid another incident.

Finished for the week, our walk home was a little more leisurely as we commiserated over what had transpired that week and since January. We knew that beyond our group of seven, all of us scrubs were becoming a more cohesive group. Our fates were tied together and, often, if one of us failed, we all suffered consequences. We had also come to understand that in terms of the outside world, there was no difference between an old guy and a scrub. If threatened by an outsider, the team responded with unanimity. It was definitely all for one and one for all. There would be hell to pay if any team member allowed physical harm to come to another without coming to his aid. The brotherhood of The Imaginary Circle was no longer a figment of our imagination; it had taken root and was growing inside each of us. Life as a scrub was no picnic, but we soldiered it through one day at a time, one pushup, one sit-up, one chest-caving punch at a time, relying more and more on each other for moral, physical, and spiritual support.

CHAPTER 6

"Malcontents"

Things would be different, we thought. At least we felt different. Something was going on internally in all of us that we had no way of measuring. We were becoming more confident of our physical selves with each passing day. Dave Young joined the team and was the newest addition to our band of scrubs. All eyes were on him the first day he walked into The Room, his reputation having preceded him. We all wondered if he would be subjected to the same level of abuse and discipline that we had been. Was there anyone who would raise his fists to punch him out? I didn't think so; none of us did. Of course any old guy had the support of the whole team, so Young couldn't get a fair fight if he were to defend himself from an aggressor. But there was one tradition they all had to contend with and it could be a deterrent to Young's suffering much physical punishment. If at any time one old guy had a problem with another old guy, he could call him out. This was a challenge to a fight in the middle of The Circle, and all requests were granted. So, who would risk being called out by Young after he turned old guy? Who would risk being called out in a fair fight with a pugilistic legend? Each one of us, though, had issues with several old guys for what we considered extremely harsh treatment and we all harbored thoughts of biding our time until we could call them out in the middle of The Circle and exact retribution.

At any rate, we felt Young would add strength to our group of twenty-one. But even without him, our strength as a group was growing, and we looked out for each other in a number of different ways. The intensity of workouts remained high, but they were not as difficult for us any more and we were all making it through each session without being harassed for dogging exercises. I was noticing how much my own individual strength had grown. My arms had developed to the point of having definable muscle, as had my legs and the rest of my body, and I had begun to walk differently, assuming an air of confidence.

The aura of protection surrounded me. Although I was subject to any number of physical challenges from within, I was shielded from physical harm from anyone outside of The Cult of the Imaginary Circle. I could go anywhere without fear, and I reveled in it, as did the rest of the scrubs.

Longer days meant longer workouts, and we looked forward to the end of school for the summer with one rather large reservation: the possibility that we were going to scrimmage all summer long on the Hill. There were of course regulations against high school football teams practicing in the summer, but as long as no coaching staff or school administrators were present, it wasn't considered official. It would be as if we had all assembled for a pickup game for our own enjoyment. The Hill was an infamous secluded area about a mile and a half from the school. It was a strange place that, if you didn't know it was there, you would never find it. Hidden by a cluster of trees and wild shrubs, the entrance lay behind a jutting mound of earth, which forced all those seeking ingress to walk a narrow path overlooking a thirty-foot cliff. Around the hilly bend laid the opening to a slightly slanting dirt surface, large enough for offensive and defensive teams to run against each other.

I cringed at the thought of scrimmaging all summer on the Hill because it brought other complications with it. Those other complications often meant working for old guys, mowing their lawns, painting their houses, cleaning their houses, or doing for them various and sundry chores their parents had given them. The only consolation was that tradition was generally followed when scrubs worked for old guys, and that meant no beatings and scrubs were usually fed. There was one incident, however, that cautioned every scrub against thoughtless tongue-wagging while in the company of old guys. Several scrubs had been working hard all morning at Moose McCoy's home when he called them inside to feed them. When they had gotten inside, Joe Martin said, "Thanks, man, I could eat anything." "Anything, hunh?" replied Moose, as he walked over to his cupboard, searching for just the right vittles to satisfy the "anything cravings" of an all-too-talkative scrub. Settling on a can of dog, food he opened it and handed Joe a fork. The phone rang and Moose left the room to answer it. When he had returned Joe had finished eating the dog food and Moose remarked, "I kinda wanted to see you eat that," and proceeded to open another can.

The decision to scrimmage on the Hill depended on how satisfied team leadership was with an assessment of team conditioning, strength, and precision while executing plays.

During the last week of school, the decision was made to scrimmage during the summer and we were informed during the final seventh-period workout. Although no scrub looked forward to scrimmaging on the Hill all summer, tradition demanded that scrubs who did were made old guys after the final scrimmage. That was the only redeeming factor.

It was deceptively cool that first morning of practice on the Hill. A pale gray hue stood motionless over everything, clouding my perception of what was about to take place. The seven of us walked slowly, with resigned determination over flattened weeds and crabgrass toward the hidden interior of the Hill. Scrubs gathered on one side of the field silently preparing for practice while an almost festive mood emanated from where old guys were getting dressed. While we were getting ready for practice, several old guys began tossing rocks at us from a pile they had stacked across the field. Shortly afterward, we were ordered closer. Taking turns, they threw rocks as if they were at a booth at an amusement park and when one of us was hit with a rock we were expected not to flinch.

After having provided the morning entertainment, it was time to begin practice and we were summoned to The Circle to hear instructions on how the scrimmage would proceed.

The second team would be up on defense against the first string offensive squad in order to work on precision plays. As the drills began, the offense walked through each play over and over again, one step at a time, to the point of which defender should be blocked or moved. Quarterback handoffs and pass plays were executed in slow motion, frame by frame. This was what we had joined the team for, serious football, and we watched, taking notes, concentrating on the positions we would eventually play. Then it all moved up a notch, a gear at a time until play execution was at full speed and blocking and hitting was at full force. It was all-inclusive except for tackling. The runner with the ball was only to be tagged with two hands to indicate a tackle.

Soon it was our turn to participate. I ran onto the field, eager to show what I had learned and the physical prowess that six months of strenuous workouts had produced for me. I was playing over the left guard position, and as the ball was snapped, I dug my heels into the loose dirt. Pushing off with all of the force my calf muscles could provide, I lunged forward, head up, left shoulder aiming for the right rib cage of the offensive guard, thrusting my left elbow toward his upper body. WOMP! His right forearm found the left side of my jaw like it had been guided there by satellite and I was driven backwards several feet. We collided over the line of scrimmage again and again with similar results. I was getting a lesson from the first string left guard that would prove valuable later on, but the point of instruction was painful to say the least.

Day after hard-hitting day we scrimmaged, we ran plays, and we walked through drill after drill until the first team's precision and skill was first rate. This was where the championship season had been created, carved out of the dust and grime and pain and the very collective soul of the team, eager for victory over any and all who dared step onto the same playing field.

The second team, in fact, could have won the championship that year, and our group of scrubs contributed significantly. We were one of the largest groups of scrubs to ever stick it out together. We had breadth and depth, size and speed, and tough determination. We performed when expected to, followed the rules, and expected to be able to rely on tradition. We looked forward to the last day of scrimmage and toward hearing the words that would make us old guys.

I kicked a rock for two blocks down the sidewalk of Hermitage Street and was amazed that I was able to keep it in front of me despite the curbs and other obstacles in my path. As I rounded the corner on Monticello Street and walked up the steps to Leo's house, boisterous noise and laughter bumped through the walls and windows and into the charged morning air. The gathering, our neighborhood crew, was having a pre- celebration before our last scrimmage as scrubs. Inside, all of my boys were hanging out, enjoying the moment.

"Hey, scrub," Leo said, stretching his hand out for five. "He ain't a scrub" Joe replied, "he's a damn-near old guy" and a sanctioning chorus of affirmation reverberated through Leo's living room as we all reveled in anticipation of old guy status.

Our attitudes, and our gaits, were upbeat as we pounded the pavement to the Hill. Reaching the field, we joined the rest of our boys and prepared to scrimmage. It was an up-tempo practice, and all of our efforts were over the top, down to the very last minute.

Gravity continued to pull the sweat off of our faces, as we stood with dirt-streaked cheeks in the after practice meeting, waiting for the final words to close the summer session. The team leaders began the meeting indicating how good the summer scrimmages were and that the next time we would be together would be in two weeks for the start of season practice.

"Oh yeah, we decided not to turn you scrubs until after the championship game,"

Charlie said, and you could have knocked us all over with the same feather. The light at the end of the tunnel had been on the front of a train that had just run us over. We felt betrayed, cheated out of what we had earned, something that had always been part of the tradition reserved for the faithful. For a second or two everything and everybody stood still. The air hung heavily over the circle we had formed, it was foul and dirty air, burning our nostrils.

Our eyes, wide in surprise soon narrowed in scowls and frowns of anger and disbelief. We walked off of the Hill in pounding silence, outraged to the point of irrationality.

"I ain't goin' for this," Peeler exclaimed, and to a man, we all agreed emphatically.

"I can't believe this," I said. "What are we gonna do now?"

"I know what to do," Leo shouted, "we need to wait here and jump them chumps one by one." Twelve of us stood venting our anger, heating up the corner.

"Okay, okay, let's go to my crib," Leo said. "We gotta talk about this."

The sidewalk heaved under our choleric footprints as we marched off to Leo's house. Resentment over a year and a half of abusive treatment had surfaced to combine with our anger at not being turned old guys. Once inside, we made efforts to curb our language out of respect for Mrs. Loar and Estella, but we spewed venom like cornered snakes. We were bound and determined to get our just due.

Half of us wanted to quit while the other half wanted to take more drastic measures; a fight to demand that we be turned old guys.

"If we all quit, they can't finish the season. They'd have to bring us back and turn us," Walker said.

"Man, they wouldn't ask us back. They don't respect nothin' but force and violence," Peeler added.

"That's right, but those cats don't respect us. We have to fight to get their respect," offered Lawrence Banks, one of the leaders of our group, who lived about a half-block from school.

"Do we want to play ball or what?" Bridges asked. "What happens to the season?"

"Right now, this ain't about football or the season," I suggested. "This is about us. I'd rather be a 'hey babe' in the stands if they don't turn us."

It had become clear to us that decisive forceful action was the only course of action to take. But it demanded consensus, an all-for-one-and-one-for-all approach. We needed a buy in from every scrub. We decided to have another meeting and left it up to Leo and Banks to contact the rest of the scrubs and arrange for an immediate gathering.

The day was gray and overcast, not unlike the cloudy mood over the large room we gathered in at Kenny's house. Most of the scrubs were there and all that weren't gave their proxy and support. We were in it together. The only scrub we weren't able to contact was Young, and his involvement would loom large for us, especially if our action were to involve a physical confrontation.

Discussion had already begun in small groups, and soon the entire room was enveloped in pocket conversation with two central themes, fight or flight. Mass resignation could hurt the season and then there was the mass migration theory. It had all of us quitting and moving to another school to play ball. That theory had its appeal to our revenge instincts. We would have the opportunity to physically oppose old guys on the field athletically but also with our knowledge of their football system and its application. But that went against the grain of everything we had believed in since we had heard the word football and Westinghouse mentioned in the same sentence. There was also the fact that we had become the products of a violent and confrontational football cult, a system designed to make us tough and fearless. Fighting was seen as the only reasonable alternative.

A calm seriousness quieted the gathering as we spoke one by one, advocating for a confrontation. If we had to fall, we would fall together, fighting. We voted to revolt and challenge what we believed had become a system that had turned on itself and had begun to consume itself from the inside out. We were making plans for what could become the bloodiest day in the history of The Room. Each one of us had an assignment, a target, an old guy to single out and beat by any available means. There would be no talk, no negotiation. We would take advantage of the element of surprise. After all, nothing like this had ever happened before. It would be like a rabbit turning on a hunter and beating him into submission with a tree branch.

We carefully assessed our strengths and weaknesses, pairing two of us against a strong target where necessary. There were twenty-one of us and seventeen of them. We had the weight and the size and the numbers to win, especially with the assistance of a few well- placed hidden boards and baseball bats. We knew that they would not hesitate to use whatever they could to defend themselves. In addition to all of what we thought we had going in our favor, we had the heart and the courage that had literally been beaten into us.

And then we had Dave Young, but we had to get word to him of our plan.

CHAPTER 7

"Gain from Pain"

In the few short days that passed between our meeting and the first day of season practice, we met and talked in small groups. Even though we were planning for an unprecedented revolt, we tried to enjoy what was left of our summer vacation. We gathered one afternoon for a basketball game in the alley behind Leo's house. It was a small space with just about enough room for a small car to pass through without scraping its sides on brick walls or other alley structures. Our basketball hoop was the top of a bushel basket that had been nailed to a telephone pole. We could have gone to a playground or a gym for better accommodations, but this court was private, insulated from the general public and insulated from old guys or other unwanted intruders.

After picking sides, the ball was thrown into play along with knees, elbows, and anything else that could be used to drive to the hoop. Our games, whether football or basketball, were always physical, and not because we were trying to prove our manhood or to test our physical endurance. We had just, plain and simple, become roughnecks.

At the height of the game someone noticed Leo's mother standing at the end of the alley waving, trying to get our attention. All play stopped and all eyes and ears were on Mrs. Loar.

"Leo, what are you gonna to do about that bird's nest?" she shouted.

"What bird's nest?" Leo asked.

"The one on top of your head, I thought you were gonna to get a haircut," she replied. Our entire crew doubled over in laughter, falling all over the alleyway. It was especially funny to us since the Loars owned the barbershop five blocks away.

Having regained our composure, it took a few minutes for the game to resume at the same level of intensity as we had displayed earlier, and a half an hour later it folded altogether. We trudged back through Leo's house, stopping in the kitchen for water. As we left the kitchen, we also left a counter full of dirty glasses and an empty water jug. Estella and Mrs. Loar deserved commendation for putting up with us and the constant traffic through their house. All of our families deserved praise, but the Loar's and the Avent's homes were our hangouts. Joe's dad, Doc Avent, was in tune with our skirmishes and exploits and often shared his insights by telling us countless stories.

We retired to one of our favorite spots, a wall about three feet high and twenty yards long, on the corner of Monticello and Collier Streets. We sat exchanging put downs of each other, a practice we called "cappin'," but for some reason that wasn't enough to satisfy our need for entertainment. Somehow the discussion turned to pro wrestling and a character that used to assail his opponents with what he called "Coco Bombs," an elbow delivered downward on the top of the head with brute force. Then a shoving match began between Walker and David Petett, the preacher's son, who didn't play football but hung out with us much of the time. Soon, Walker was choking Petett to the point of near unconsciousness until Petett squeaked out a cry for help. Leo decided to assist and Coco Bombed Clifford Walker's head so hard that it momentarily stunned him and us. Walker, grimacing in pain, grabbed his head with both hands while we offered a chorus of ooos and aws in between spurts of laughter.

"What's wrong with you, man?" he yelled as he rushed forward in an effort to extract an apology in the form of Leo's head hitting the pavement. As they began to wrestle on the sidewalk, half of us tried to intervene while the other half tried to prevent the intervention. We rolled out into the street, interrupting the flow of traffic and the neighborhood peace. Rumbles between us, fortunately, were devoid of deep-seated anger, fists to the face, kicking, or biting. Everything else, however, was standard, including but not limited to fists to the chest, headlocks, body slams, and of course Coco Bombs. This rumble was one of our most notorious, lasting a full ten or fifteen minutes and sprawling at least a half a block and back while neighbors just shook their heads at our ruffian-like behavior.

Exhausted, we gradually returned to the wall to boast over who got whipped and who did the whipping. Shortly, though, our conversation turned to comparing notes on who had the best shot at the finest girls in school. That was just about all we could do as scrubs. The fact that we were not allowed to date or have a girlfriend was a definite deterrent, and exceptions were extremely rare.

It was getting late, and we all left in order to get home before curfew. It seemed so strange to still abide by the rules while we were planning a revolt. But the reality was that we wanted to uphold all of the traditions. We still continued to be practitioners of the order of The Circle and were willing to fight to keep the faith into which we had been indoctrinated. At home, my parents noticed a difference in my behavior. They felt that something was wrong, but my total denial and tight lip about what was going on just barely got me by. It was identical to what my brethren were going through.

Friday morning, the last weekday before our planned confrontation, arrived under an overcast sky, which was not unusual for Pittsburgh. The mountains, trapping clouds and pollution from the steel mills often gave us a big gray tent to live under. After doing a few chores, I bathed, dressed, and was on my way out of the house when the phone rang.

"Hey, Reed, this is Leo. It's off, man. Somehow the school found out and there was a police car parked outside of The Room all morning. Everybody is on the way over here now."

"What," I asked in shock? "How could they have found out?"

"I don't know," he answered "that's what everybody wants to know. Anyway, I got to call Bridges and Peeler. See you when you get here."

I jumped down the steps in front of my house four at a time and headed to Leo's. If what he told me was true, what alternative would we have, I thought? Would we all have to quit and transfer to another school in order to play ball? Leo's living room filled up quickly and overflowed into the dining room with large bodies and big feet.

"Man, somebody dropped a dime on us," I exclaimed. "How else could they have found out?"

"I heard that somebody's mother overheard some talk about our plan and called the coach," replied Lawrence Banks. "And that ain't all," he continued, "I just heard that they turned Dave Young and made him first string center."

Our mouths fell open simultaneously. This meant that now as an old guy Young was a part of the group that we were planning to confront. We all figured that the intention was to take away our most potent weapon and point it at us at the same time. We had also lost the element of surprise and, without it and Young, our plan had become seriously flawed.

And then there was the squad car, what significance did it have? Someone had also heard that the police were seen coming out of The Room with the coach and walking around to the back of the building. It was decision time again, but the situation had changed. We had unanswered questions. How much did they know? Did all of the old guys know?

If we decided to stick it out to the end of the season, would there be repercussions as a result of our failed attempt to revolt? One thing was certain; we had to pull Young into the discussion to see where he stood and what his allegiances would be. What would he do if a fight broke out anyway?

We couldn't delay our decision until we talked to him. It had to be made before the meeting broke up. It was Friday and season practice would start at eight Monday morning, and we had to make sure that all of us were on the same page. At that point, at that quintessential moment, we all discovered how much we loved the game and wanted to play football for Westinghouse. We decided to show up for practice as though nothing had happened, as though we had never made plans to revolt and go along with the program unless we were singled out or attacked.

It was late Saturday afternoon and, as we sat on the Collier Street wall, Dave Young walked across the street. We were all curious as to what had been said to him and how he was told that he had been turned.

"What's goin' on fellas?" asked Young in his typically understated style. He knew what was up and that we all would be interested in what his position would be. We listened intently as he began to speak. He had not known of our plan to revolt. We had not gotten to him in time before he had been turned. Had he known it would all have been different, but he assured us that our relationship with him would not change. He would look out for us, and although he could not keep us from being harassed, he would not stand by and let anyone hurt us. Young thought that with just about three months left we ought to stick it out, after all this was the season, the reason we all had gone through the pain and misery. The logic cut clearly through the angst and uncertainty but did nothing for our disillusion.

"Hey, man, we scrimmaged all summer on The Hill and they shoulda turned us. They're wrong," Bridges said.

"And you scrubbed for a year and a half. The hard part is behind you. All you have left is about three months and then you can settle the score. This is the season. This is what you joined for," answered Young.

We were hard pressed to dispute his reasoning, but we were angry, disenchanted, and frustrated: still every one of us decided to continue.

Somber would have been a festive description of our mood as we walked to school for that first practice. The August sun, taking advantage of a cloudless powder blue sky beamed down unfettered heat. "That's just what we need," someone said, "its gonna be smokin' hot on the field." The open shadeless field was little more than a hundred yards of dirt that often gave up much of its composition in the form of dust.

In an effort to keep the dust down, the field was regularly oiled and a fresh new coat was already bubbling up. We knew that by the time that we hit the field the sun would have heated the oil to a blistering degree. The air was tense and our jaws were tight as we filed through The Room door and took our seats on the benches in the scrub section. Surprisingly, both coaches were there and remained while we dressed in full pads and they stayed for the practice meeting. Their presence avoided any type of confrontation, and no one even mentioned our failed plan to revolt.

Over the fence, down the hill and onto the field in helmets, cleats, and full pads, the whole team circled up for warm-up exercises. We jogged in place and then jumped down for pushups, the worst exercise to do on a hot oiled field. Blistered hands were the norm rather than the exception, and no one wanted to stand up with oil or dirt on their jersey or knees, a clear indication of dogging. The only relief came by momentarily shifting to fingertips or by lifting one hand off of the surface for a split second. Regrouping on the sidelines for a quick meeting, the offensive and defensive starting squads prepared for full-contact scrimmage, for a hard-hitting, tackling, everything-goes square off.

It was a rough morning. It was a long morning. It was a take-no-prisoners, no-one- escapes unscathed morning. Everyone hit hard, and everyone was hit hard. The first team offensive unit took a beating, so much so that the afternoon practice was not a scrimmage. We practiced in shorts, shirts, and cleats, an unheard of event for an August practice.

The end of the day was very much like the beginning, with the coaches in The Room as we dressed, and no reference was made to either our plan for revolution or our discontent. Tired, sore, and carrying a blister or two, we trudged home recalling the day's events. Even though we had gotten no resolution of our problem, there was definite satisfaction over our performance on the field during scrimmage and definite gain from the definite pain.

CHAPTER 8

"The Two-Helmet Meeting"

Blisteringly hot, contentious, and constantly under the ever-watchful eye of the coaching staff only partially describes the seriousness of football practice during August. And each day was very much like the first. Remarkably, no one brought up our plan to rebel, and we didn't speak of our discontent, although it seethed just below the surface. I had a sneaking suspicion that some way, somehow they would try and punish us. The Order was not known for benevolence. There was occasional harassment and physical abuse during those tense days of August, and whenever it happened, the angst was universal for scrubs. We all stood tight-jawed, feeling the pain of our suffering compadre, and all just one punch, one hurt, one injustice from exploding, from giving as good as we were getting.

Fortunately, for the most part, everyone's attention was focused on playing football. A couple of scrubs made the first string defensive squad, including House Hardy. Named so for his massive size, he was the biggest player on the team.

Physical and tough, House earned a reputation in the mean streets of the Larimer Avenue area of town.

Legend had it that at an earlier age he used to stand at one end of the Larimer Avenue Bridge charging a fee to anyone who wanted to cross to the other side. His intimidating size and manner would serve him and the team very well as defensive tackle. The rest of us would get the opportunity to play as either a part of second or third string teams depending on the score of the game.

As tradition had it, varsity scrubs also comprised the junior varsity first team offensive and defensive squads, and we were going to have the opportunity to play a good bit of football during the season. Westinghouse ran a single wing offensive formation which had an unbalanced line and was a powerful running offense with pulling guards and tackles. In the single wing formation, the left side of the center was light, comprised of only the left guard and the left end. The right guard, inside and outside tackles, and the right end lined up to the right of the center.

I played inside tackle on offense and left tackle on defense and, at one hundred and sixty pounds, I was small for the position but didn't have the speed for other positions. Admittedly, I wasn't the greatest ball player in the world, average with a spurt of excellence here and there. I was, however, like my boys, able to handle the extreme exercise and conditioning and able to tolerate the intimidation and physical mistreatment. With The Imaginary Circle Gang, strength under pressure, courage in the face of adversity, a stoic, tight-lipped attitude, and blind faith counted more than anything else.

The last day or two of preschool practice was filled with team assignments and execution drills on both offense and defense. We were all relieved to see them end and the new school year begin. I was excited to be entering the year as a sophomore and officially as a member of the varsity football team. I remember swelling up with pride that first game day as I walked into school with my Bulldog Jersey on and especially when several of us walked the hallways to class together. Our games were always held on Fridays and, on the day of the game there were pep rallies with the entire team on stage in the auditorium. Seated on stage with the rest of the team, it was difficult to hold back the beaming smile behind the blank face, but the customary solemnity and game day reverence was mandated.

Something could certainly be said for the safety of riding a bus in full football pads and helmets, but it was offset by the discomfort, especially if one sat next to a super-sized lineman. But that was secondary to the elation of riding the varsity bus to a preseason game against Mt. Lebanon, an upper division suburban school. This was our second preseason game.

We had lost the first game against Aliquippa six to zero. Our preseason games were against schools outside the city league we played in, and those teams were usually much bigger and much better financed organizations. Mt. Lebanon was the quintessence of that model. It was a wealthy school in a wealthy white upper class community. We were amazed at the appointments in the huge gleaming locker room we were allowed to use as the visiting team, individual lockers, smooth unsplintered benches, shiny, freshly painted floors, water fountains, and showers fit for corporate executives. We could only imagine what the home team locker room looked like. The experience of running out onto manicured grass that they called a football field was equally amazing, and its size was only surpassed by its luxury.

During warm-up exercises, a flash of yellow light caught my eye, and I glanced in its direction. It was coming from the reflection of stadium lights off of the shiny rims of tubas in Mt. Lebanon's marching band. The tuba section was ten deep in what seemed like a never-ending procession of band members numbering in the hundreds in crisp, flashy uniforms. The gleam from what looked like spank brand new instruments was enough to light up Homewood Avenue on a dark moonless night. The size and accoutrements of Westinghouse's band paled in comparison. There were several instruments so old and so faded that they seemed to disappear under the white light from stadium lighting fixtures. However, when it became time to perform, Westinghouse was outstanding, making up for what it lacked in numbers and flashy new uniforms and instruments. While continuing to enjoy a first-class reputation in the region, the band was the perfect complement to our football program.

This game against Mt. Lebanon was seen as a tune up for season play. All of the preseason games were, especially since we continued to play teams out of our league, teams with five-and-six deep coaching staffs and deep bench strength in most positions. It almost made us wonder why these teams wanted to play us, but we were, in fact, a city dynasty, winning, in sixteen years, fourteen out of sixteen city championship titles and six in a row. We were known to be aggressive, extremely hard-hitting, fast in the open field, and unapologetically willing to remove an opponent's head from his shoulders.

The stands were full of thousands of people; many that came to see Mt. Lebanon beat the mighty Bulldogs. We kicked off to Mt. Lebanon, and they returned it to the ten-yard line. On the next play, they fumbled the ball, and we recovered it near the twenty-yard line. Our single wing offense lined up and on a rough count, "ready, down, set," snapped the ball. The right tackle pulled and, behind him, bolting up the middle for twenty yards and the touch down was our halfback John Brewer.

We fought the good fight aggressively throughout the game and upset Mt. Lebanon twelve to six. Our preseason schedule was a good tune up for the regular season. School administrators could have put together a schedule that included teams from schools closer to our size and with smaller sports budgets but it would not have gotten us ready for city league play, where everybody wanted to knock us off.

As we prepared for the regular season, another breach of the tradition and trust of The Order occurred that threatened to turn the season upside down again. The Ritual of Golden Gloves was reserved for newly turned old guys and was observed during the off season. During the ritual, GG, as it was known, opponents were chosen like gladiators to fight bare knuckles in The Circle, and fighters were often selected who were friends or who had some type of bond. This made for a more sadistic backdrop for the tournament. Bloodshed was mandated. Fights were to be as if combatants disliked each other or had an ax to grind. The infliction of pain was demanded, and punishment was issued for non-competitive or docile matches.

On the day that the ritual was to be observed, we got word of the intent. We also heard that old guys were seen dragging pipes and sticks into The Room. I never found out who had pulled our coat to the intentions, but I always thought that Dave Young was somehow connected, living up to his vow not to let anyone hurt us. It would have been in accordance with his sense of justice. Word spread quickly to all but four of us, and we decided to quit en masse. The Circle Gang was caught off guard and fortunately did nothing to the four uninformed scrubs that showed up for practice. Our actions stirred things up enough to have the team send negotiators out to recruit us back into the fold. They scoured the streets but were not able to find enough of us to come back to practice. We empowered Leo and Banks to negotiate for us. We were not going to comply, no Golden Gloves until after we had been turned old guys and not until the off season.

We summarized that old guys had planned to retaliate for our planned revolt and the Golden Gloves Ritual was a ruse. We knew that, had we complied, there would have been some other insidious action to punish us for our earlier insolence, for not cowering to the absolute control of old guys who were subverting long-standing tradition. Finally, the ritual was postponed, a truce was declared, and we returned to The Room. The regular season began and we dominated City league play as expected. We could feel the title in our bones. This would be yet another year for Westinghouse to win the championship and make it seven years in a row.

It was a warm Friday afternoon, and we were poised for a home game against Schenley High School, another predominantly black school in the Hill District of Pittsburgh. Schenley's team had developed into a formidable adversary that was not going to be a push over. It had been stressed at our meetings during the week that Schenley had been performing well and talking trash about what they were going to do to us on our home field. We all knew that it was going to be a tough grind but we were ready willing and able to face and defeat them.

Game day arrived and the first half was very tough, and we were letting their offense move the ball too easily up and down the field. The score was too close for comfort and tempers flared. House Hardy had been playing defense opposite one of Schenley's star offensive lineman, a big, rough, trash-talker who had prevented him from penetrating the line and making tackles. The first half drew to a close with a still unimpressive showing for our team of grunting Bulldogs. We retired to the small field house for our halftime meeting. It was a tiny space we were crammed in like a size twelve foot in an eight and a half shoe. After the coach read us the riot act, he turned to exit and slowly squeezed through the sweating mass of bodies and equipment. As the coach left he shut the door behind him, and for a half of a minute or so no one spoke. The field house fell silent but for the sound of Charlie gnashing his teeth as he paced the tiny open space in the toy-like building.

He was pacing with his helmet in his hand, gesturing emphatically with it as though it were an extension of his arm. He paced over to where House was sitting and stopped squarely in front of him.

"House, you ain't hittin, man," he shouted and with his hand on the face guard of the helmet, swung it backward then up in a swift, wide arch and crashed it down on the top of House's head with enough force to have knocked out the average prize fighter. He slammed his helmet down on the top of House's head again with equally damaging force. The sound was loud enough to be heard outside of the field house.

No one moved. Our eyes bugged out as House reeled in pain, barely able to keep from falling off of the bench. The irony of it all was that it could not have taken place anywhere else in the world. House would have snapped anyone else in two for violating his body in such a manner. The act had the desirable effect. It got everyone's attention. Charlie promised that we would all be lucky to be able walk home after the game if the second half proceeded like the first. The team left the field house resolute. There would be no taking of prisoners during the second half. We jogged back onto the field with new resolve and determination. House was mad enough to crush rocks with his bare hands and was anxious to get back onto the field.

The second half began ostensibly enough as Schenley received the kickoff and returned the ball to their thirty-yard line. Our defensive team ran onto the field, and House took his position over the offensive tackle. As the ball was snapped, House raised up from a three point stance, fiercely crashed through the line and tackled the fullback in the backfield. Shouts of approval and encouragement reverberated from the stands and sidelines. Schenley decided to test House's resolve and on the second snap from center ran the play straight at him. They had planned to double team him and run the ball over the top of him. But it wasn't happening. House stood up in the hole pushing both offensive linemen backwards and, reaching out with one hand, pulled the fullback down with a crushing thud.

From that point on, House put on an awesome display of defensive hitting and tackling. He washed the field with Schenley's lineman who had bested him in the first half and forced the ball carriers to the other side of the field to avoid him. On one play, it appeared as though half of Schenley's line had caved under the pressure of a hard-charging House Hardy.

Suffice it to say, we won the game and it was partially due to the defensive exhibition that House put on after the two-helmet meeting. All of us scrubs were buoyed by House's performance, but we were also unappreciative of the corporal punishment he suffered at half time. We took it personally, but we understood that performance was mandated in the Cult of the Imaginary Circle.

CHAPTER 9

"A Turn for Champions"

The Schenley game pulled our coattails. We were good; we were tough; but we could be beaten, and if it happened, there would be hell to pay. Our next challenge would prove to be the toughest game in our quest for the city title. We would play South Hills, a school not known to be competitive against us. We had beaten them by thirty points or more each of the last four years. Their coach had been an assistant coach with Westinghouse for a number of years before coaching for South Hills. He was keenly aware of our offensive program and understood every play in our arsenal. South Hills was ready for us and fought us tooth and nail, but our physical conditioning and determination proved to be too much for them to overcome. But we won the game by one measly point.

The scene in the locker room was tense and fractious as tempers flared. The team's performance was well below par, and no one escaped blame. Even those who didn't play were given a portion of the burden to bear. Winning by one point was not appreciated. It was seen as a failure to execute and dominate. It was interpreted as a sign of weakness.

An announcement was made that first team offensive and defensive players were to stay for a late meeting. This kind of meeting often meant fist fights as each individual player answered for his performance or lack thereof. This also meant that practice for the next week would be very intense and physically strenuous even though the next team on the schedule was considered a real lightweight. But after the last game, it didn't matter what team we played. The message registered loud and clear that everyone's performance had better be over the top. The week began with a fierce scrimmage. Every player on the roster felt the brunt of the last week's narrow victory. It was one of the most demanding scrimmages in our history, but we benefited from the sheer physicality of it. The shared pain was a bonding experience that brought us all closer together, scrubs and old guys alike. We were becoming seamless.

Game day arrived and we were pumped. Opportunity was knocking, and we were answering with every fiber in our bodies. Our opponent, South High, (different from South Hills), was going to feel the power of momentum and witness the manifestation of destiny. The game was to be played at home, and the field had been made ready with extra attention paid to detail since it would be the last varsity home game of the season. The moment arrived for us to take the field, and we charged down onto the surface with all cylinders firing, roaring with enthusiasm. We won the coin toss and from the opening kickoff began to control every aspect of the game, special teams, offense, and defense. The score quickly rose to twenty-eight to nothing, which meant that we would all have the opportunity to get in some quality time on the field. In fact, it became one of my best performances at defensive tackle, breaking into the backfield on one play and sacking the quarterback for a ten-yard loss. The final score of the game was fifty-five to nothing and team spirit and camaraderie had never been higher. There was only one varsity game and one junior varsity game left in the season. We were so close to the championship game that harassment from old guys was almost nonexistent. Everyone was more interested in winning the city title and nothing else mattered.

The sense of purpose was so strong and omnipresent that it was beginning to blur the line between old guy and scrub.

Time jumped by and the day of the last junior varsity game was upon us. It was also our last junior varsity home game, and a small crowd of die-hard fans showed up to watch. We expected to win as did just about everyone else in Homewood. We took control of the game from the very beginning, marched down the field toward the goal line and huddled up for a third down play. The play called was a power play straight up the middle of the field with the ball carrier running to my right. It required me to block the lineman directly in front of me and drive him to my left. The ball was snapped and I dug my toes into the dirt, driving the defensive tackle out of the hole, and the ball carrier powered over the line of scrimmage. After the back ran past me, I released from my block to follow downfield. Our ball carrier was stopped, and I was a part of the pile up of bodies on the twenty-yard line. As I was pulling myself out of the pile, one of the opposing team's linemen was standing directly over me with his back toward me and the pile.

He was huge, at least three hundred pounds, and to one of our players, he presented an opportunity to release some pent up hostility. Our guy had been approaching from the other side of the field, charging like a rogue bull elephant. When he reached the light obliterating mass of flesh and football gear hovering above me, he lowered his head and lowered the boom. I heard an ugly sound, an all too familiar sound, a sound that usually meant that someone was going to be hurt. And then it came crashing down on me, that gathering of weight and equipment, that enormous collection of humanity, obeying the laws of gravity and motion. I tried desperately to get out of the way, to avoid being flattened like a pancake.

I succeeded in removing most of my body from danger but my left arm remained in the path of destruction and was the recipient of blunt force trauma, snapping like a twig under the tire of a cruising Greyhound Bus. I was momentarily pinned to the earth until someone pushed the great quantity of humanity off of me. I rolled over and struggled to my feet. My left arm hung motionless at my side. I lifted it up with my right hand and it swung like a scarecrow's arm in a mild meadow breeze. The pain began to throb as I turned and yelled to my boys who were already back in the huddle.

"Hey, look at my arm," I yelled. I was surprised, but shouldn't have been, when I heard,

"Aint nothin' wrong with your arm, punk, get in the huddle."

"Hurry up Reed, before we get a penalty."

I digested the pain and, with disregard for common sense and my personal well-being, walked into the huddle. The next play was a pass to the right flap requiring me to protect the passer and prevent line penetration. When I reached the line of scrimmage and bent down to assume a three-point stance I had to place my left arm on my left leg with my right hand. After the ball was snapped, I lunged forward and threw a right forearm into the chest of the defensive tackle playing in front of me. He of course threw a right forearm at me and hit the upper part of my left arm. The pain shot through my entire body as we struggled over the line of scrimmage. The pass was completed in the end zone and we kicked the extra point. I was also playing on special teams and, after the extra point, lined up for the kickoff.

I played the entire quarter with a broken arm until the junior varsity coach began to make substitutions. When I reached the sidelines I removed my helmet and doubled over in pain. I stood up and walked over to where Mike Turner was standing, held up my arm and asked him how it looked. The expression on his face spoke volumes.

"Man, you should show the coach," he said in an alarming tone.

"Does it look that bad? I asked.

"It ain't that good, man, you gotta show the coach." I walked over to the coach and showed him my arm. Without pause he pointed across the field and told me to get the assistant athletic director to take me to the hospital. I started to walk down the sideline to go around and up the steps, but he stopped me and told me to go straight across the field and then up the steps. As soon as I walked onto the field the referee blew the whistle and called a penalty on our team for having too many men on the field. I could hear my boys complaining in disbelief that I was walking across the field while the ball was in play, broken arm and all. And these were scrubs; there wasn't an old guy in sight. The line between old guy and scrub was blurred no longer. At least in demeanor, we had become them. As tight as we were, it made no difference when it came to football. The game had become foremost in our lives. We held no one and nothing above it. The cult was powerful, taking over our lives and ensuring it would live on in us. It had insinuated itself inside of us as though we were a host body and it was benefiting from a symbiotic relationship.

Reaching the hospital, the assistant athletic director dropped me off and left. He evidently assumed his duty done, having gotten me to the entrance of the hospital emergency room. I walked in, still in all of my football gear and cleats and spoke to a nurse about my arm. They put me in a wheelchair and pushed me to an interior hallway. I sat in that hallway for over an hour with nothing for the pain, no solace, only the piercing twang of country music wailing from a loud radio two rooms away. It must have truly been my unlucky day because the doctor they sent to help me was the most inept, incompetent physician I would ever come in contact with. The first thing he did was to grab my arm and manipulate it as though it were not connected to the rest of my body. I was cooperative until it just got out of hand.

"Oh that must hurt," he grunted.

"Do you know what you're doin?" I asked as I pushed him away from me and sat up on the exam table.

He stood silently scratching his chin and then decided to send me to get x-rays. After my x-rays were reviewed, I was sent to surgery to have the bones set in my arm. I remember them telling me to count backwards on the operating table but I could remember little else. The operation was supposedly successful, but bringing me out of surgery and down in the elevator to the recovery room was a different matter. Apparently, while in the netherworld between unconsciousness and consciousness I was back on the football field yelling at the top of my lungs, "Saaay now, heyyy now." I was trying to get up off of the table, and they couldn't hold me down. There were two orderlies and a nurse trying to keep me from jumping onto the floor. The orderlies were trying to hold my arms down, and the nurse was trying to hold my legs down. I kicked the nurse back to the elevator doors and, as she was sliding down to the floor, I shoved one of the orderlies against the wall. By then, the elevator had reached the recovery room floor and the doors opened. My dad had been standing there waiting for them to bring me down from the operating room. I know it must have looked like a scene straight out of bizzaro world, but he quickly stepped in and, with his help, they managed to hold me down long enough to get restraints on me until I woke up.

I was amazed and a little spooked when I learned what had happened. I realized that the rituals of The Imaginary Circle had become so deeply a part of me that, even under the effects of anesthesia, I was subject to their influence. I didn't spend much time in the hospital or recuperating at home and was back at school a couple of days later. I had missed the last game of the season against Peabody, but we defeated them without much difficulty.

The only game remaining was the battle for the city title against Langley High. The mood of the team was guardedly optimistic but the customary solemn tone and focus prevailed. There were only five days left until all scrubs were turned old guys after the championship game, and we could hardly contain ourselves. We were being treated like human beings. We suffered no abuse, and practice was serious and to the point, a matter of business. We all had one mission, finish the season as champions of the City of Pittsburgh High School League. Our unity of purpose was so strong that anything not directly connected to winning this last game was seen as frivolous and intolerable.

Langley was a team to be reckoned with. They had a tough defensive squad that had allowed few points to be scored against them in league play. Their quarterback was flashy and had gained quite a bit of notoriety. He was quick and had a rifle arm that was accurate to forty yards. They had a run-and-gun offense, and there was talk all over town that this was the match up that the league was salivating over. The hype was fueling everyone's expectations, and we were selling wolf tickets all over town. It was finally upon us, the day of liberation and victory. Just about everyone in Homewood was eager with anticipation, and the atmosphere in school was electric, especially since our opponent was being touted as the one team that could knock us off. All championship games were night games, and the after parties and celebrations were both famous and infamous. We would celebrate in a manner only allowed once a year and only after winning the city title. That night was the only night we were allowed to drink alcohol and smoke. Of course, it was done without the knowledge of school or coaching staff and our parents. There would be none of them with us on the bus coming back from the game, and that's where we hid our cache of wine, whiskey and cigars for our postgame celebration.

The bus ride to the game was quiet, with little talk other than what needed to be done to execute the game plan. It was difficult holding the excitement inside. After all, this was it. This was what it was all about. This was what we endured the tortuous physical conditioning and abuse for. This was the ultimate test of our will to dominate. By the time we were ready to leave the locker room, we were pumped up beyond belief. I felt the same enthusiasm and anxiety as every player on the squad. Even though my arm was in a cast and I was still a scrub, this was to also be my night of liberation. We charged out onto the field fiercely, hell bent on destroying Langley High.

Langley received the ball first and their flashy, hot shot quarterback sauntered out onto the field with their much-ballyhooed offensive unit.

The air was crisp, supercharged, and sound reverberated throughout the stadium. This was a night for us to reign supreme. This was the first time we had ever played Langley and, from the onset, we intimidated them. We were the legend they were coming face to face with and we talked stuff from the very first play, putting the fear of defeat in their hearts. Langley snapped the ball. The quarterback took several steps back looking for an open receiver and, finding none, turned up field to run, all to no avail. He was brought down at the line of scrimmage with a resounding thud loud enough to draw a chorus of "ooos," from the crowd. On the next play, our defense hit so hard that the Langley backfield folded from the weight of its own linemen. We shut them down, and they were forced to punt; and we returned the ball to midfield.

We scored on the first series of downs, and it was all over but the shoutin'. We held them scoreless throughout the entire game. We totally dominated all aspects of the game and the final score was twenty-seven to nothing. Westinghouse was top dog again, and it was time to celebrate. We had been liberated. We were old guys at last, free to rejoin the world of regular people again. At the moment of freedom, however, we all felt something extraordinary. All of the resentment we had held for two years vanished. We accepted all of the team with open arms. We had no desire to challenge those who had beaten and humiliated us. There was no hatred for our tormentors, no urge to retaliate for what they had put us through. There was only a great feeling of well-being and brotherhood. We embraced each other, congratulating ourselves for winning the championship, and those of us who had just turned old guys were congratulated for sticking it out, for making it through the toughest physical and emotional regimen in the country for teenagers. Many had been called but few had been chosen. It was time to celebrate. Taking a shower after a game, a real shower under hot water gushing from a showerhead and using soap was a new experience for newly turned old guys. After dressing, the team packed the gear away on the equipment van and headed to the team bus. We had a system for drinking on the bus. It was done at the back of the bus behind a couple of guys standing in the isle blocking the view of the driver, and we consumed until the bus pulled into the schoolyard.

It was traditional for hundreds of people to meet the team bus back at the school to share in the celebration. It was also traditional for the team to exit the bus through a gauntlet of girls who hugged and kissed the players. It was euphoric leaving the bus as an old guy and a champion and to receive the adoration of so many appreciative young girls.

Life was good again, and all was right with the world.

CHAPTER 10

"Fate Twists"

My attitude about everything had changed. I was a member of the most prestigious organization of teenagers in the city of Pittsburgh and was under its umbrella of protection and influence. Life as an old guy called for immediate adjustments. The return of the ability to do all of the things that regular teenagers could do brought a new appreciation for what most of them took for granted. I could wear decent clothes to school and pursue the affections of any girl who would tolerate my advances. Lunch was a reality again, and just being able to walk into the cafeteria and stand in line with other students seemed like a real treat. On my first day back in the cafeteria line, I stood waiting with Estella Loar who couldn't help but chuckle at my enthusiasm for school lunch food. The aroma of the daily special, meatloaf with mashed potatoes and gravy, was intoxicating and I drooled in eager anticipation.

There was no one to hide from and no one to fear, and I piled my tray up with enough food for two people. Estella was amazed at the amount of food on my tray as we walked to a table to sit and eat.

"Either you're expectin' someone else to share your lunch or you're expectin' a baby," she said, as we squeezed in between several other students at a crowded table.

"I'm expectin' to make up for every lunch that I missed as a scrub," I said as I scarfed down every bit of grub on my tray. Lunchtime, which used to drag by as we hid in our secret spaces as scrubs, darted by, and Stell and I were walking back to class together as I shared with her the latest joke going around school. She had the funniest laugh I had ever heard. It started like a stifled sneeze behind her nasal cavity and the more tickled she got the worse it got, resembling rapid fire from a muffled machine gun until it finally burst through uncontrollably. She and I were becoming close and were forming the foundation of a solid friendship, one that would allow us to spend many hours together.

I was beginning to get used to wearing a cast on my arm as Christmas vacation rolled around and all of our neighborhood crew were making plans to party with reckless abandon. On the first Friday that we were off, there were two parties in Belmar Gardens, a small residential community located on the top of one of Homewood's hilliest areas. Seven of us, all newly turned old guys, overjoyed at the reality of our first night out partying in over two years, trekked up Brushton Avenue towards Belmar Gardens with David Petett. The first party was at Judy Ralph's house, and when we reached her front yard, three of us decided to scout out the other party, three blocks down the hill.

About an hour later, we got a call to arms, a call for the reservists, a call for back up at the other party. Apparently, several guys had threatened our boys with bodily harm. We were told that the party was breaking up and there was going to be a confrontation in the front yard. There were six of them to three of our boys, which made them believe that they could win if a fight broke out. Getting the message, we all, including Petett, bolted through Judy's door and down the steepest hill in Belmar Gardens at breakneck speed. A crowd was gathering in the street in front of the second party, and the instigators were standing in front of our boys selling wolf tickets. Halfway down the hill, we could see everyone milling around in the street. We felt like the cavalry charging into battle, and when we came into view of the bystanders, someone yelled, "Hey, here comes some more."

The six of them turned and, when they saw us approaching, took off in several directions. Two of them were caught immediately and were stomped in front of the circling crowd, while another ran toward his front door with Leo Loar in close pursuit. Unfortunately for him, Leo was a track speedster and as the guy jumped up two short steps and extended his hand for the screen door, Leo reached out for him with both hands, swung him around, and up and body slammed him in the matted, winterized grass of his front yard. For a second or two, I had a season flashback to when Leo caught a fleeing halfback bolting down the sidelines at full speed and slammed him in front of the bleachers so hard that his body bounced a foot and a half off of the hard dirt field.

After the brief rumble, we walked back up the hill to Judy's party where we were among trusted friends, and when we entered her door, she let us know that she would be the only one throwing punches in her house. "Don't make me have to call your momma," she exclaimed as she pointed her finger at us. There would be no trouble at Judy's house. She was dating Chicken, (Leslie Griggs) who lived in the heart of our little neighborhood, and although he didn't play football, was considered as one of our boys. In fact, we hung out with several guys in our neighborhood that didn't play ball including David Petett and Chicken. There was Jimmy Moore (Blake), and Fulton Berry, the gentle giant at six-feet-five inches tall and big enough to make anybody's front line offensive or defensive squad. We also hung with Kelso Gordon, tall and ultra-slim like a human Daddy Long Legs spider, and Monty Lee, also known as Homer Domer and Chrome Dome. If you were ever caught in a rock throwing fight, Homer was the one person you wanted on your side. He could pick a fly off of the top of a car antenna with a rock at fifty yards.

There were also a couple of other cats we hung out with from other parts of town like the nefarious Lenny Bailey from the Larimer Avenue area known for his sarcastic wit and Robert Riley who had a patent on an infectious laugh. Johnny Yandel was another one of our neighborhood crew. He was a big, tough, and a very talented football player who played for Peabody High School, one of our rivals in the City League. We often hung out at his house listening to jazz on his dad's stereo.

His father, a big man at six feet four or five and three hundred-plus pounds, was an avid jazz fan and had an extensive collection. Like most other black teenagers, we loved R&B music, but we began listening to jazz at the early ages of eleven and twelve and, by the time that we were fifteen, we were hard-core enthusiasts. We used to sneak into the Crawford Grill in the Hill District of Pittsburgh on Saturday afternoons to listen to live jazz. We would enter through the side door and grab a seat at a booth in the back and order a glass of iced tea and a club sandwich. As long as we stayed back there and didn't bother anybody or try to walk into the bar area, we were left alone. We were truly initiated fans and were devotees of the music of John Coltrane; Miles Davis; Horace Silver; Oscar Brown Jr.; Art Blakey and The Jazz Messengers; and The Modern Jazz Quartet to name a few.

We pinched pennies to buy albums and, as we sat listening to the music, we read the liner notes on the back of the cover. They offered a wealth of information about the individual tracks and the lives of the musicians. An album was a treasure trove of music and information that we discussed and familiarized ourselves with. We often read *Downbeat*, which was a popular jazz magazine that helped us gain additional insights about the music we loved. We frequently took the blindfold tests like those administered in the magazine and had gotten fairly good at it. We could listen to a new piece of music without any information and identify many of the musicians laying down tracks.

The new semester rolled around quickly, and the start of our conditioning season began with the traditional seventh-period workout sessions. I was still walking around with my arm in a cast and was exempted from working out with the team. It was also the time for new scrubs to enter the program and as they filed in The Room one by one, scraping the edges of the benches along the outer edges of The Imaginary Circle, I couldn't help but recall my first day in The Room. I looked curiously for outward signs of fear in their faces, bugged eyes, dry mouths, and nervous twitches. Most of them had found a spot on the floor upon which to fix their gaze to prevent eye contact with any of us. I knew that the physical conditioning would be just as difficult for them as it had been for all those that had preceded them. That fact was a given and part of the reputation upon which The Room had stood for more than a decade. The traditional rules and foundation for scrub life would remain the same and would be enforced diligently, but I wasn't so sure about the beatings and psychological harassment. I wondered how our newly turned group of old guys would deal with this new group of scrubs. There were still a few sadistic guys around who deserved to be feared and still others with the potential to be brutal. George "Spider" Web and Elmer "Bootsy" Goodson were the new leaders of the team and they laid down the law as others had before and assured every scrub that they had to abide by the rules or suffer the consequences. After the edict, it was time for the first workout, and as everyone emerged from The Room, my questions were answered as old guys took the first opportunity to pummel the bodies of new scrubs with fists and elbows.

Once in the gym, the team circled up for what was to be a grueling exercise session. Web was in superb shape, and he led a workout that old guys had difficulty keeping up with, let alone scrubs who were unaccustomed to such rigorous demands. They faltered and mental notes were taken, and once back in The Room, scrubs paid the price for dogging exercises. After several examples were made, they were given ten seconds to get dressed and out. As someone counted down the time, metal football hangers were thrown, crashing on the wall behind them. Hurrying and partially dressed, they bolted for the door but had to pass through the standard gauntlet of fists and elbows before exiting out into the hallway. At that point, it looked as though those scrubs would go through the same things that each group experienced before them, but to what extent was still not clear as we began our march toward another championship season.

Still in a cast on my left arm, I continued to play the saxophone in band and take lessons on Saturdays like I had done since the fifth grade. My instructor was one of the first chairs of the Pittsburgh Wind Symphony and tutored by way of classical music standards. I had gotten very good at it and could instantly sight-read any music put before me and was often asked to play difficult passages of music for other instrument sections in orchestra classes. Orchestra was the last class before lunch and, on one particular day after putting my horn away, I joined my boys who were already hanging out at one of our favorite hallway spots. We were standing against the wall when a couple of scrubs casually strolled by on their way to who knows where. Apparently they hadn't heard that it was absolutely necessary to avoid contact with old guys during lunch periods. We decided to make them aware of what could happen on those chance encounters. We called them over to interrogate and generally harass them. I had just unwrapped a piece of gum and put it in my mouth to chew but suddenly decided that I wanted one of these scrubs to keep the wrapper for me. I told one of them, Bernie, to take it, save it, and give it back to me unwrinkled, after seventh-period workout. He took the wrapper, and after my boys finished with the other scrub, we let them go. On their way down the hall, we all noticed that Bernie had taken the wrapper, balled it up and thrown it on the floor in front of a hallway water fountain.

"Aw, man, he just chumped you, Reed. He threw away your wrapper," Lawrence Banks said.

"You know what that means," Peeler exclaimed. "He ain't showin' you no respect man. You gotta make him pay." It was seen as a challenge, not only to me but also to all of my boys standing with me, and it would be up me to make the proper response.

After what had been a very tough workout during seventh period, everyone returned to The Room and scrubs were told to dress quickly and get out, but there was some unfinished business to attend to. I walked over to the door and locked it and then walked through The Circle to pick up an old tennis shoe that had been lying on the windowsill near the exterior door. I turned, walked directly to Bernie and asked, "Where's my gum wrapper, man?"

"I don't know," he said nonchalantly.

"I know what you did with it. You threw it away," I continued and before he could answer I raised the tennis shoe up and brought the sole down across the side of his face hard enough to snap his head sideways. I hit him three times across his face until there was no doubt in anyone's mind that I would respond violently if tested. Then I threw the tennis shoe against the wall.

"The next time I tell any of you scrubs to do something, you better do it."

But I wasn't prepared for what would happen next. As we stood there face to face, I saw the same hatred for me in his eyes that I felt for old guys who beat and harassed me when I was a scrub. I felt the anger and disdain for me swelling up in him and sensed an immediate ill will from the rest of the scrubs. I knew that he wanted to take a swing at me and, with my one arm in a cast, he thought that he could take me down with no sweat. But with my boys only a few feet away, it would have been a foolish undertaking. So, he did what every other scrub had done before him and restrained himself from reacting. But I didn't enjoy what I had just done. Even though it brought an instant level of respect from scrubs and regard from my fellow old guys, it didn't make me feel good about myself and it became the first and last time I harassed any of the scrubs.

The next few weeks flowed by smoothly enough, even though I was anxious to join my boys in workouts and other team activities that my broken arm prohibited. As much as we all disliked the tough conditioning program, we all enjoyed the hard bodies it produced and the superiority it gave us over teams that faced us on the football field. Because I was having difficulty generating new bone growth, my broken arm wasn't healing. Although it hadn't healed, my doctor removed the cast and placed it in a splint. I still couldn't participate in workouts or scrimmages and the weeks slowly dragged by until the first of May was upon us.

On a wet, dreary, boring Saturday night, I stood in my front doorway peering out through the screen door at the pouring rain. My sister, Ann, was upstairs hurriedly getting dressed to go to a James Brown concert, while Smokey Robinson and the Miracles streamed from our living room stereo. Running out of the rain and onto the porch, two of Ann's friends, wet and out of breath, knocked on the screen door. Ann quickly joined them in the living room and soon the three of them dashed down the steps under the still-heavy downpour and into their waiting car.

They disappeared into the wet-dark night, and I plopped down on our couch after dropping a handful of records onto the stereo spindle. About fifteen minutes later, I was still sitting on the sofa, deep in thought when the telephone rang in what seemed like startlingly loud tones. I jumped to my feet and crossed the living room floor in two or three steps and lifted the receiver to my ear. A shaky and sobbing voice on the other end spoke in broken sentences about a car accident involving my sister and her friends and urged us to get to the hospital as quickly as possible. With my heart beating like an electrified bass drum, I ran up the steps to tell my mother about what had happened. I'll never forget the expression on her face when I told her what I had just heard. I had never seen her frightened and shaken like that before.

"Oh, my God, your father. We have to call him right away," she said, and immediately reached for the phone.

He was playing cards at his brother's home a short distance away and was devastated at the news. He rushed home to pick us up and together we sped over the same wet streets that Ann had traveled a short while ago. Finally reaching the hospital, we rushed through the emergency room doors and into a gut-wrenching scene. There wasn't a dry eye in the place.

My mother and father immediately conferenced with the doctors about Ann's condition. Although I was out of earshot of the conversation, I was close enough to see the expression on my parents' faces and to read their body language. My mother gasped and covered her face with her hand as she leaned on my father's shoulder. They had been told that Ann's condition was critical, that she had been rushed into emergency surgery, and wasn't expected to live. It would be several hours before they would have a clearer picture of her prognosis. As we sat in the waiting room, the somber details of the accident came to light through tearful accounts of those also riding in the car. They suffered cuts and bruises but weren't hurt badly enough to have been admitted to the hospital.

As we had initially heard, the car in which they had been riding was traveling at normal speed over wet streetcar tracks and had gotten thrown into the path of an oncoming car from the opposite direction. Ann had been riding in the middle of the front seat; Vernon Thompson had been riding next to her in the front passenger seat and the right front of the car suffered the brunt of the collision. Vernon didn't survive the crash and was pronounced dead on arrival at the hospital. Pittsburgh streets were famous for their narrowness, and those with streetcar traffic were no exception. They were usually full of parked cars on both sides and traffic moving in both directions. The metal streetcar tracks, with a several-inch groove in the middle of each track were infamous for catching car tires and making the car swerve left or right. When they were wet, the effect of the swerve could be multiplied many times over.

The Thompson family, shattered and deeply hurt, huddled, commiserating over their terrible loss. There were very few words that could mitigate their grief, only time and prayer could heal a wound so deep. Nevertheless, they waited with us, eager to learn of Ann's condition. We all sat for what seemed like an eternity until her surgeons slowly pushed through the swinging doors of the waiting room with expressions of deep concern covering their faces. The surgery went well enough, but the surgeons couldn't promise anything. Ann's condition was still critical and she would be sent to intensive care where the next twenty-four hours would be crucial to her recovery. She had sustained head injuries with severe damage to her neck, and even with the successful surgical procedure, the doctor's couldn't determine her prognosis. While it wasn't good news, it gave us hope, hope that would be joined by many prayers and direct conversation with God.

Then the real waiting began, and if time had seemed to drag before, it now seemed to edge backwards with each tic of the clock as we sat outside the intensive care unit. After what felt like an eternity, the morning sun, filtered by partially drawn shades, leaned out into the hallway and my mother decided to call my other sister to fill her in on the horrible details of the last night. Janet was devastated by the news and caught a ride home from school to join us at keeping a vigil at Ann's bedside. She stayed until late Sunday night and then returned to school for the week. Ann was still in intensive care, and her condition had improved but not enough for the doctors to change her prognosis. By the end of the next week, however, she had been taken off of the critical list and moved to a semi-private room; and two weeks later she was well enough to be discharged. She was in a neck brace and was to remain in bed, getting up only with help to go to the bathroom and then back to bed again.

Janet came back home that weekend from college to help with Ann, and we were all breathing a sigh of relief except for the fact that my dad was not feeling well and had passed out at work during the week. His doctor couldn't find anything wrong with him and sent him home to rest. Janet was due back at school for class on Monday, and my dad would have driven her back but he was still not feeling well and was still resting in bed. My parents asked my Uncle Ollie to drive her back to school, and my cousins Ollie, Jr.; Kat; and I went along for the ride. The drive up to California State Teachers College was uneventful and after dropping off Janet with hugs and well wishes, we pushed off for home. The night was dark but clear as we made our way back over highway unlit but for an occasional oncoming headlight of a car or two. We were all in a calm but pensive mood, and I had been gazing out of the window up at the night sky. We rounded a bend in the highway, and a strange celestial presence caught my eye.

Up above it all, but beneath the moon and the stars, a dark gray patch of fog and mist hovered over a weird looking clump of trees and low lying hills. I followed it with a fixed gaze until it disappeared behind a hilly clump of tall, barren trees. I didn't know what to make of it because although it wasn't unexplainable as a phenomenon, it had such an eerie presence.

An hour or so later, we were back home and my uncle dropped me off and rolled on because Monday was an early workday for him. Once inside the house, I ran upstairs to tell my mother that everything went well and to see how my dad and Ann were doing. My dad was still under the weather, and Ann, although no better, was at least no worse.

I grabbed a quick bite to eat and then climbed into bed. Several hours later, in the middle of the night, I was awakened by my mother's panicked voice calling me. I rushed to her bedside, still foggy from a deep sleep.

"It's your father. I think he's having a heart attack. Massage his chest while I call an ambulance."

My eyes were wide open then as the blood pumped wildly through my veins and my brain shot adrenaline blasts through out my body. I climbed onto the bed and began massaging my dad's chest. He appeared to not be able to catch his breath and, in fact, his breathing had stopped. My mother and I continued in vain to revive him as he literally died in our arms. By the time that the ambulance had gotten to our house, he had been dead for ten minutes and my mother was overcome with tears and shock. I went to Ann's bedroom to tell her what had happened, fearful of what the news might do to her already delicate condition. She erupted in tears and tried to get out of bed, but I convinced her that there was nothing she could do and that getting up could make her condition worse.

I turned to go back to my parents' bedroom, but the ambulance crew was emerging with my dad's covered body on a stretcher. I sat on top of the dirty clothes hamper in the tiny space between bedrooms and closed my eyes in disbelief as they passed me and struggled down the sixteen narrow steps from our second floor. Seconds later, I opened my eyes to see my dad's lifeless body disappear through our kitchen at the bottom of the stairs. I went into the bedroom and sat next to my mother and put my arm around her to comfort her, but there was little solace that I could offer. We had just been through a terrifying and shocking experience, and it was just too soon for comfort.

After immeasurable anguish and tears, the morning sun peaked over the horizon and fell through the dining room window, and into the darkest moment of my young life. My mother had been on the phone talking to Janet about what had just happened. The shattering news left her sobbing in shock as she gathered a few things together to return home immediately to be with us. While my mother was on the phone with my Aunt Velma, I opened the front door and walked out onto our porch. Lawrence Rembert was crossing the street, headed for school, when he saw me standing on the porch.

"Hey, man, you goin' to school or what?" he asked.

"No," I answered, "my dad died this morning."

Stunned, he ran across the street and up the steps.

"What happened?" he asked, and as I related the details, he shook his head in disbelief. He offered his sympathies and while the two of us were talking, Art Davis appeared, walking down Brushton Avenue.

"Hey what's goin' on?" he asked and when I gave him the news, he joined Lawrence and me on the porch, and the three of us stood there talking long enough to make them late for school. They offered to stay with me and help in any way possible, but there wasn't much they could do at that point. A few hours later Janet, arrived home under a great deal of stress. It was good to have her back. The family had shrunk to four, and we all needed each other to get through our ordeal.

Soon, the whole community knew, and there was an outpouring of sympathy. The efforts of all of my boys helped to keep me strong. The Imaginary Circle Gang closed ranks behind me in support. The next few days crawled by slowly until the day my dad's funeral was upon us. The church was full, and my boys took up several pews in the back.

As sad and tearful as the service was, I struggled to keep my eyes dry to present a front of calm and strength for my mother and sisters. After all, I was to assume the role of protector, the "man of the family." Tears welled up in back of the tough wall that had been raised between my emotions and the outside world during my tenure as a scrub. Grief, anger, and resentment all crashed my wall as I labored to deal with the tragedy of the death of my father and life, as we knew it then.

CHAPTER 11

"Fixed, Frozen, Shocked"

Several days later and back at Westinghouse, I tried to resume the normal routine of high school life. But I soon came to understand that life had changed, had become abnormal, and that nothing would be the same anymore. It was so much more serious than I had ever realized before. I had been forced to deal with a series of events that I could never have prepared for and that, unbeknownst to me, were only part and parcel of what was to come. Hanging out with my boys helped to put me in a different frame of mind as the last few weeks of school before summer vacation dripped by like thick muddy water through a pin hole leak in a clogged rain gutter.

Because my broken arm hadn't healed yet, I stood by as the team exercised during seventh period and had no desire to participate in the harassment of scrubs, who had been joined by a new recruit from Peabody High School. Billy Vasser, a talented, able-bodied running back transferred to Westinghouse when his family had moved to within a few blocks of the school.

Vasser was a fierce competitor who wanted to win and relished the opportunity to play for a championship-bound team. He had a reputation as an excellent ball player, but was also known for giving a good accounting of himself in a fistfight. He was regarded as skillful and somewhat legendary in the streets, but he was not prone to instigation. He was generally known to be rather calm and collected and one to avoid a fight. It was odd I thought, but most of the guys I knew who were extremely proficient as street fighters, and in a class by themselves, were outwardly cool and much of the time risk averse. It just didn't seem to follow. Then there was Dip; another legend and a friend who was the same way, recognized for his skill in a street fight and who trouble seemed to find. I finally reasoned that after so many fights building a reputation, these guys had grown weary and wanted to enjoy a little peace. There were, of course, those of lesser skill that always seemed eager to make a reputation for themselves as they challenged the fastest hands in the community.

Billy Vasser's transfer to Westinghouse was seen as a good thing, but he would have to scrub right along with all of the other new guys interested in making the team and submit his body to the rigors of our conditioning program. As we wrapped up the last seventh- period workout, plans were made to scrimmage on the Hill during the summer, but without scrubs. We had enough coverage in each position to run a full team on offense and defense.

Scrimmages were in the late afternoons, and I spent the early part of the day on chores around the exterior of my house before finding something else to do. As usual, after scrimmages were over, we often wound up sitting on the wall on Collier Street and Monticello, or shooting the breeze at someone's crib. One afternoon as we sat around Joe's living room, someone called someone else a punk, and a spontaneous wrestling match erupted until a foot crashed through the dining room wall leaving a hole the size of a cantaloupe.

"Doc is gonna kill you, Joe," I said, walking closer to the wall. Joe was frozen in disbelief, which was soon followed by a tirade blaming all of us for his predicament. We all helped to straighten things back to where they were before the match, but we all knew that when his parents got home and found out what happened that he would be sentenced to the crib with numerous menial chores to perform. After we left, Joe finished straightening up but decided to go one better by immaculately cleaning up the downstairs; then he placed one of the dining room chairs against the wall to cover the hole. When his parents got home, they were astonished at the cleanliness of the living room, vacuumed rug and all, but they smelled a rat. They knew that something was up and as soon as Mrs. Avent walked into the dining room, she questioned the out-of-place dining room chair. Joe was thinking on his feet and tried to sit in it to prevent discovery of the gouge in the wall. But before he could reach it, she had it in her hands and his cover was blown. He spent a couple of weeks in lock down for that incident, but it was nothing new, however, to the chronicles of Joe Avent and parental discipline.

Doc Avent was famous for sentencing Joe to house arrest for his foibles. There was the time when Joe's family was ready to eat dinner and needed a loaf of bread. His mother sent him to the local store two blocks away, told him to hurry, and admonished him not to stop at Leo's on the way to or from. Of course, he stopped at Leo's both on the way to the store and on the way back. By the time he had reached home again not only was dinner over, but the dishes had been cleaned, put away, and his family was watching television in the living room. On top of that, the loaf of bread was unrecognizable as such and had been rendered inedible from the role it had played as a football in Joe's hands. Mrs. Avent was livid as she wrested the suffering dough from under Joe's sweaty armpit. He received a light sentence for that, however, but the record was a whopping forty-four days on lock down for an incident related to groceries he had been told to carry into the house. Doc had told Joe to bring in a case of dog food and to put it in the basement. He stopped short of the basement and deposited it in the middle of the third step down. After several days and several warnings to remove the case of dog food from the steps, and after Doc nearly broke his neck falling over it, Joe began serving time.

Perhaps the most infamous incident occurred when Joe's two younger sisters were home alone, and he sneaked into the house without them knowing it. He rattled silverware in the kitchen drawers and made noise like a burglar while speaking loud enough for them to hear.

"Hey, you get the TV and I'll get the radio. Keep lookin' for some money." He scared his sisters to the point of their hiding in the closet hoping that the burglars would not find them. Then he left home again and his parents found his sisters hiding in the closet when they returned. When they told their parents what had happened the Avents knew who the culprit was. Joe received and served out a sentence in solitary confinement.

My older sister, Janet, was home for the summer, and Ann was recovering nicely from her brush with death. The preceding months of agonizing time pulled my abbreviated family closer together than we had ever been as we commiserated over the loss of my father and tried to move on. We continued our tradition of eating dinner together and attending church on Sundays, holding onto each other and our faith. Many days of bright yellow sun rising over the bushy tops of hillside trees and laughing young children punctuated the remnants of summer, and soon both of my sisters were packing for college, and I was looking forward to the fall semester of school and the new football season.

As the September session began, the team was poised for another victorious season, and I gradually began to get back into the rhythm of normalcy. Walking the hallways with my arm still in splints gave rise to so many questions that I thought of wearing a sign saying, "Yes, it's still broken." Some of my boys even started calling me "broken arm." It was obvious that I was not going to play any ball during the season, and I worked the sidelines trying to inspire the team on to victory as we rolled on confidently and fearlessly. We felt as though we were prepared for any eventuality and when the day arrived to play Peabody High School, we welcomed the challenge. This game would be the defining moment of the season. Johnny Yandell and his dad had been selling wolf tickets for days and they were anxious for the clash. We were playing without our star defensive lineman, however; House Hardy, who had injured his knee, was out for perhaps the rest of the season.

The atmosphere was absolutely electric, and charged air crackled over the school and everything in close proximity as we jumped over the fence and ran down the hill onto the field. The team looked good, we felt good; the fans were excited and the whole community cheered us on, but as the action on the field unfolded, both our offense and defense faltered. Something was wrong, something didn't feel right, and our unbeatable drive stalled in neutral. And there wasn't one reason that we could put our fingers on; there were many. The once charged-air now stood like heavy water over the field and stands as we struggled for four quarters. Time was running out and the score was tied.

Our quarterback dropped back for a pass and fired a bullet spiral intended for our receiver sprinting down the right side of the field when Johnny Yandell jumped higher than even he thought possible, and intercepted the ball. And then, like a charging rhino, no, like a possessed charging rhino at full stride, he raced down the sideline toward the goal. He was unstoppable and scoring a touchdown pushed Peabody into the lead for the first time in the game. From that point on, everything was absolutely surreal. It was as if we had become spectators at our own demise. Nothing worked; we had hit the wall. An eerie silence fell over the crowd; every footstep, every grunt, every block, every tackle was magnified tenfold. It was a scene made for the "Twilight Zone" as the final gun signaled the end of the game and the end of an amazing winning streak. We all stood like department store mannequins, fixed, frozen, and shocked, in utter disbelief. It was a nightmare, and we were all dreaming it awake. Peabody's team was ecstatic, and the few Peabody fans that had come to the game were cautiously overjoyed, careful not to overstate our loss and their unimaginable victory.

We gathered at the far side of the field, appalled over the loss of a city conference game and our performance as a team. This had never happened during any of our tenure with the team, and no one knew what to do. Webb spoke in a distressed tone and Bootsie Goodson admonished us to go straight across the field, up the steps, and to say nothing until inside The Room.

As we gathered ourselves for our exit the silence was so strange because it was the first time the team had ever moved without the background vocals of scrubs. We made our way past the bleachers, and our fans, whose tears were enough to muddy the field. Once we were all inside and the door locked, all hell broke lose.

Skirmishes and accusations over who didn't perform and who did erupted everywhere, and scrubs feared for their natural lives. If the coach hadn't unlocked the door and entered, who knows what might have happened?

He calmed us down and told us to just get dressed and to go straight home. He remained in The Room until all of us were gone. The walk home was an unforgettable dirge. We were angry and in utter shock over losing to what we had considered an inferior team and the stain it would leave on our record. Surprisingly enough, we harbored no ill will toward Johnny Yandell or his father. Peabody had beaten us fair and square, and if we had to lose to somebody, at least it was to a team that one of our boys played for. It was also a vindication for Mr. Yandell, because he tried for years for a coaching position at Westinghouse. He even tried to become involved as a volunteer with the coaching staff, all to no avail. Had he been able to participate, Johnny Yandell would have undoubtedly played for us. There was only one black coach at Westinghouse, a predominantly black high school and that was the track coach. In fact, there were precious few black teachers or black administrative staff or even black janitorial staff at Westinghouse. In short there was very little opportunity for black folk to work there.

We were angry, though, over the loss, angry with ourselves. We had no one else to blame and for the first time that I knew of, we had doubts about the future of the team. This loss caused us all to question our preparedness and abilities. Finally, near home, I climbed the steps and, when I opened the door, my mother asked me about the game. I could hardly get the words out of my down-turned mouth.

"We lost," I muttered and dived onto the couch and buried my head in a pillow.

"It's only a game," she said, "and there'll be many more." But whatever tomorrow would bring there would be no joy that night; mighty Westinghouse had lost a season game for the first time since who knew when.

The next day was no better and, in fact, was worse as I dragged myself out of bed and downstairs for breakfast, only to see the newspaper full of what was deemed to be an upset of historic proportion. The news media was all over the story. There were a lot of people in other parts of the city who were all too happy to learn of Peabody's win over Westinghouse on its home field. It was a story that was told over and over during the next two weeks. We learned that if it were difficult living up to a great reputation, it was even harder living down its loss.

The coming days and weeks would test our resolve and our character. The school scene was somber and most, except for a handful of students and teachers, were devastated at the stunning upset. We still had an outside shot at the city title if Peabody lost one of its games and we won all of the rest of ours and, strangely enough, that scenario came to pass. That meant a rematch for the chance to play for the city title, but we were swimming upstream against a powerful current of twisted fate, a fate whose irony would not be revealed for yet another year. Our efforts, valiant and unrelenting, brought us to a tied score at the close of the fourth quarter in the playoff game against Peabody.

We were prepared for a sudden-death playoff period when, much to our chagrin, the coach signaled for us to stand down as he, Peabody's coach, and the referees conferenced in the middle of the field. We questioned what there was to talk about. Sudden-death playoffs were a common way for tied teams to determine a sure winner. Our coach slowly walked back toward our sideline and huddled the team up for a meeting, but before he could say anything we heard Peabody's team erupt with screams and leaps of joy. With the score still tied, we wondered what they could be so happy about. Then the coach told us that he had agreed to decide the winner of the game by comparing the number of first downs within the twenty-yard line, and Peabody had one more than we did. Amid moans and groans we questioned selecting a statistical method of determining the winner rather than a sudden-death period. Our fans were in complete confusion as they saw Peabody's team erupt in jubilation. Gradually, word filtered through the crowd crushing the heart of our student body.

That was it, the end of the season and, for the first time in many years, Westinghouse would not be playing for the city championship. The irony was too deep for Billy Vasser. The very year he transferred from Peabody to Westinghouse became the first time in recent history that Peabody defeated Westinghouse and moved on to play for the city championship title. These events were absolutely surreal. To have our season ended by a statistical method rather than a gladiator-style death by first point battle seemed to be unsportsman like conduct. But we had had ample opportunity to take what we wanted and had failed to do so, twice.

Days and weeks after the second loss in the same season to Peabody found us all in deep valleys of depression as we licked our wounds and contemplated our future. We had a chink in our armor that we would wear until we redeemed ourselves with another city title.

Seeking solace in distraction and frivolous pursuits led me to a party one Friday night that added an exceptional dimension to my life. I walked down the steps into the basement of the home of a friend who was throwing a party and was immediately smitten with a pretty young stranger standing with her hand over her heart in the middle of a small chalk-drawn circle. She was being initiated into a sorority and had been instructed to remain there for a half of an hour. She was what we referred to as "a high yellow chick with blow hair." Her good looks, her impish smile, and the sultry flick of her gorgeous eyelids smote me.

I watched several guys trying to hit on her without success and decided to take another approach. I circulated the party without paying obvious attention to her while I took note of her every movement with my peripheral vision. But before I could develop my master plan, she was swept up by a group of girls and headed for what was a rather long ride home to the other side of town. As soon as she left, I diligently pursued her vital statistics. Her name was Veronica Rickmond; everyone called her Vonnie and she was from the south side of Pittsburgh, which was all of the way downtown across the river through the Liberty Tunnel and up the side of a mountainous hill. For days afterward, I bugged a friend, Carol Crawford, for her phone number until she finally gave in. But not before letting me know that the competition was fierce and that Vonnie was hotly pursued by no less than a throng of would-be suitors and was currently going steady with a handsome college basketball star. Not one to shrink from a challenge, I shrugged off her concerns, assuring her that it was undeniable kismet. Committed to the quest for Vonnie's affections, I secluded myself at home and dialed her number for our first real contact. I had her at a bit of a disadvantage because she hadn't met me and knew nothing about me. I was pleasantly surprised at the ease of our first conversation and the fact that it lasted for three hours. We talked like we had known each other for years, and it was as if I had been talking to Estella or Jeanie or Cookie.

The time flew by and neither of us realized that we had been talking that long. We agreed to talk again soon and said goodbye. I sat quietly digesting what had transpired and reflecting over how I had first laid eyes on her and the unique circumstances of her being forced to stand in the middle of a circle as part of an initiation into an organization. This coincidence, no matter how slight, to my two years as a scrub within the Imaginary Circle convinced me that indeed the hand of fate was at work pulling us together.

Meanwhile, back in The Room it was time for the rites of passage for newly turned old guys. That rite, the traditional Golden Gloves, was fought by every newly turned old guy upon the beginning of the new conditioning season in January. The pairings assumed the normal pattern of either friends or those closely matched in size and skill. The bare knuckle, no-holds-barred events were bloody and often injurious. Of particular interest was the match that Billy Vasser would fight. Everyone had heard about his reputation and was eager to watch. It was a quick match, and we were all impressed with his hand speed and how easily he dominated the fight until the team captain signaled its end. GG day left many bruised and bloody, but they all breathed a sigh of relief that it was over, and soon afterward, the team settled in on the task of recapturing the championship title. We would have to be better than we had ever been before and be in better physical and mental condition.

Things were really different. Most of our neighborhood crew was no longer in The Room. They were graduating and were through playing football. Art Davis had already graduated and was attending Bethune Cookman College. Lawrence Rembert was graduating in February, getting married, and moving to Cleveland. George Webb was graduating in February and would be attending Thiel College. Leo Loar, Clifford Walker, Malcolm Jones, and Michael Peeler were all graduating in June and were entering the Air Force. The three of us left; Joe Avent, Albert Bridges and I were forced to think about the immediate future and what we might be doing after graduation.

I was more focused on my broken arm. My mother and I had become convinced that the doctor that had been treating me was totally inept and we took another course. We found two new doctors who were surgeons. They decided to do a bone graft, which meant that they would remove bone from my hip and graft it onto the fractured spot on my left arm. They scheduled me for surgery and, in a few weeks, I went under the knife again. I was facing the reality that I might not ever play ball again, and my doctors weren't making any promises. They put a pin in my arm to hold the fracture together and weren't sure about my ability to play during the next season. I recuperated at home for a week and then returned to school, unsure about the future but at least convinced that my mother and I had made the right decision.

The team was still hard at work conditioning for a bull rush at the city title. We all wanted redemption in the worst way and were bound and determined to avenge the devastating loss to Peabody. The likelihood of my not being a part of that effort became a crushing reality after meeting with my doctors several weeks later. After reviewing x-rays, they said that the pin would have to stay in my arm and the splints remain on until well into the season. I would not practice or travel with the team and would not officially be a member of The Imaginary Circle, but once an old guy, always an old guy. The bond would never be broken and I would still be regarded as one of the boys.

The thought did occur, though, that this could be the best of both possible worlds. I could enjoy the status that came along with the team and hang out in the stands with all of the honeys that followed the team. In short, I was destined to become a "hey-babe" with the status of a jock.

Vonnie and I were getting closer with each telephone call but had not met eyeball to eyeball. My boys questioned the worth of all of the time I had spent talking to a chick on the telephone without getting much more from it than conversation, but Vonnie and I were becoming friends, and I had become addicted to our dialogue. Of course, I had other ideas about our relationship and continued to chip away at her resistance one day at a time, but she was still involved with the college sophomore she had been going steady with and refused to invite me to visit her. I knew, however, that it would be just a matter of time before we would become much closer, and I had other pursuits to occupy my interests. I had crushes on two other girls: Melba Scott, who sat next to me in homeroom, and Vicky Mosely, to whom I often wrote poetry. And there was another mystery chick I met one weekend who left an indelible impression on me. It was late on a Friday night, and I was headed to the Penn Shady Ballroom known for hosting great dances that attracted huge crowds from all over the city. There was always someone new to encounter there and, on this night, there would be someone special.

By the time I had arrived, the place was packed and the dance was in its final half-hour. After circumnavigating the joint, I found a few of my boys hanging out near the front entrance and stopped to shoot the breeze with them until I noticed a vision of loveliness standing alone nearby. Perfect get-acquainted music began to seep slowly out of the speakers overhead. I walked over to where she was radiating a warm glow and asked her if she would like to dance. Her cold, jet-black eyes froze mine at first glance and her wicked smile framed by moist fleshy, lips flashed a warning sign that I chose to ignore. Without speaking, she reached for my hand and we headed for a space on the dance floor.

She had the softest skin I had ever been lucky enough to touch and it looked like purified honey. This would be no ordinary encounter I thought as I held her hand and maneuvered to the perfect spot on the dance floor. I pulled her tender young body as close to mine as the law, would allow while we slow dragged under dimmed lights and the spell of sensual soul music wafting out of the ballroom sound system.

I was close enough to feel her heart beating beneath the tight knit sweater she was wearing that fit like it had been sewn on before she left home. "What's your name?" I asked. "Sshhh," she replied in my ear with sweet-hot breath I could almost taste as she gently placed her perfumed, pliant cheek next to mine. We both closed our eyes as we floated through time, space and music made for dreams. Rarely had life opened the doors to its enchanted garden, but for a few magical moments, we were ushered in. If there were ever an opportunity to freeze time and make the moment last forever, this was it, with a pretty young seductress in my arms and nothing else on my mind.

But the inevitability of ever-moving time ended our tryst. As the music stopped, we reluctantly separated and she smiled at me and then whispered in my ear: "You'd better leave me alone."

I smiled back at her partly out of confusion and partly out of instinct. Before I could speak, two of her friends were pulling on her arm.

"Come on, girl, our ride is here," they said, almost in unison. As she was being pulled away, she looked back, smiled, waved, and disappeared into the crowd and out into the deepening blue-black night.

That was the beginning of an on-again off-again thing that existed only on the dance floor and continued for several months. I would find her at a dance and we would share several brief moments together, but our relationship never advanced beyond our enchanted dance floor embraces. It was strange but compelling and we both looked for each other and enjoyed what felt like pristine snatches of perfect time. I had no objections and regarded it as something to look forward to on a Friday night in Pittsburgh.

But soon even that disappeared as our paths failed to cross at the big dances and she remained the real mystery chick of my youth.

All of these things and my solid friendship with girls like Barbara Brown, whom I had also known since grade school, and the fact that I was fortunate enough to remain close to Estella, were helping me to continue to gain insights into what the opposite sex was really like.

So, my world had become full of women and I was loving every moment of it.

CHAPTER 12

"One Day…and It Won't Be Long"

This was it, the last year of school at Westinghouse. I was a senior and, although I looked forward to graduating and moving on, I was enjoying each and every day. There was literally nothing else to do during the day except go to school. All of my friends were either in school or had graduated and were in college or the service or had moved away from Pittsburgh. There were only a few students who had chosen to drop out of school and Westinghouse was the happening place to be. The general idea was that we might as well get an education and try to have fun while doing it. Our parents would not have allowed us to drop out of school, and we generally did what our "raise," as we had begun to call them, wanted us to do. "Raise," of course, was slang, and our word for parents because they raised us. We not only respected our "raise" but everybody else's. They had an invisible will that blanketed the community and kept us all in line. We wanted to do what they thought was right. There was a bond that existed between the community elders and its youth.

This was an exciting time, the beginning of a new football season, one in which we were determined to redeem last year's loss, and it was the beginning of the end of an era. I was becoming more aware of the inevitability of change and that no one was promised tomorrow. I was beginning to understand that no matter how badly I wanted something or how much I thought that I deserved it, some things just weren't meant to be.

However, that didn't apply to Vonnie Rickmond. I was convinced that she had to be the rule rather than the exception. My dedication and persistence had finally paid off. She had finally agreed to see me and I was going to make the creep on Saturday night.

A creep was what we called visiting a girl at her home, and it was something that we prepared for religiously.

We believed in the importance of being well rehearsed and prided ourselves in our ability to "rap," to talk our way in and out of anything. The oral tradition was strong in the black community in Pittsburgh and for one to have a lull in the conversation, a blank spot where there was nothing to say was a cardinal sin. The conversation had to be smooth and effortless or you risked the loss of cool points. We all had a repertoire to fit a number of occasions, but Doug Baskins was especially known for his smoothly cool jargon. Someone asked him one day if he was playing about something he had said and he replied, "Hey, I don't play. I threw my radio away yesterday cause it played." As one who was well rehearsed, his lexicon was quotable and became a part of the spoken word tradition of the community. When asked how he was doing, he was known to say, "I'm just hangin' around town with a brown frown, tryin' to git down," or, "I'm fair for a square from Delaware."

Since we were such jazz enthusiasts, jazz played an important part in a creep. Each jazz album had its own story from the music itself with particular passages of brilliance and detail to the members of the group and their personal style and history illuminated in the liner notes on the back of the album cover. We prepared for a creep by selecting an armful of albums to take and decided upon which one to start and end with and where to make comments. It all depended upon the mood we wanted to create. With a stack of albums under my arm and a three-and-a-half-inch brim on my head tilted at a ninety-degree angle over my right eye, I set off on my journey across town.

I strolled into Vonnie's yard and up the steps onto her porch as cool as I knew how to be and rang her doorbell. Her father answered the door, stared me in the eye with a what-are-you-doing-on-my-doorstep look on his face and waited for a response from me.

"Hi, Mr. Rickmond, is Vonnie home?" I asked as politely and as respectfully as possible.

"And who are you, young man?" he asked, without opening the screen door.

"I'm Frank Reed, she, ah, she knew that I was comin' over," I replied. He gave me the once over look again and opened the screen door and invited me inside.

"Have a seat," he said and disappeared to tell Vonnie I was there.

Momentarily, Vonnie bounced into the room, with her hair in a pony-tail, a sparkle in her eyes, and flashing the same dangerously sweet and sexy smile that melted my heart the first time I laid eyes on her.

"Hey, what's that under your arm?" she inquired.

"Some of the best music you'll ever hear," I assured her, as I reached for what had to have been the best place to begin our musical interlude. It was Miles Davis' "Someday My Prince Will Come;" a classic that contained one of John Coltrane's most beautiful tenor saxophone solos on a cut called "Teo."

Vonnie's receptivity and eagerness to listen not only to the music playing on her stereo, but also to my play-by-play commentary reassured me. She was gracious and made me feel comfortable in her home. Soon, the conversation flowed like water over Niagara Falls, as did the time. I couldn't believe that three and half-hours had passed so fast, so completely unnoticed by either of us. When Vonnie and I talked, time seemed to be irrelevant except as a starting and ending point for our connections, the middle of which was always deliciously rich and playful. Our interlude ended on a high note, and I was soon home reflecting on the evening and vowing to continue to pursue the elusive Vonnie Rickmond.

A bright September sun warmed old tired bleachers on an early fall afternoon, and I was in the stands again with the rest of the students. It felt like a completely different experience watching my boys from across the field and not being a formal part of the team. This was the fourth time, however, after sitting through preseason play, which ended with Westinghouse winning two out of three games. The team had performed well and appeared to be on track for another championship year. Although I felt a twinge of melancholy or rather, separation anxiety from The Cult of the Imaginary Circle, there were enough distractions to keep me pacified.

The stands were packed with girls I knew and wanted to get to know, and excitement and enthusiasm charged the air. The band was decked out in crisp blue and gold and six coquettes in gold sweaters and short blue skirts kicked up their heels, cheering us on. Vicky Mosley was a part of the cheerleading squad and although the crush I had on her never generated any more than a poem or two and a good friendship, her presence always excited me.

However, on the other hand, Eleanor Harris was standing right next to me, and I didn't know what to make of my feelings for her or how to characterize our relationship. We were friends, of course, but the short snatches of time that we spent together were encounters of the future kind. They were like glimpses of what it was going to be like to be with a truly captivating woman, and Eleanor was every bit of a woman, sophisticated well beyond her teenage years. Smooth, sumptuous, and blemish-free brown skin, come-hither eyes, a heavenly body, and a sassy attitude that said look, but don't touch, made me like a young pup in her presence. My gift of conversation and knowledge gleaned from early friendships with Jeanie Harriston and Cookie Sloan allowed me to get closer to Eleanor than most of the other tongue-wagging high school puppies around. It was not uncommon for us to walk hand in hand down the hallways of Westinghouse and when she kissed me on the cheek as we parted to go to class, my status in the dog pound rose significantly. But our relationship never went much further than that.

A few rows up and over were Gail Austin, (who went to Schenley High School) and Martha Roberts, and when the three of us got together, we stretched the boundaries of sanity to the extreme. Mike Turner, who dropped from the football program after playing junior varsity ball, and his girlfriend, Stuff, were sitting directly in front of me. Her nickname had always intrigued me and made me want to ask how and why she had gotten it. However, I was more content to leave the reasons up to my imagination. I tapped Mike on the shoulder and raised the sleeve of my shirt and showed him my cast-free, splint-free left arm that had finally healed but, unfortunately, too late for me to take advantage of the football season.

"Wow, Frank, when did you get the splints off?" He asked.

"Yesterday," I answered, holding my arm up for all to see, prompting a round of applause from a whole section of bleachers.

Our attention focused on the field as the opening kickoff ensued and Westinghouse quickly established its dominance from one end of the field to the other. It was as though we were all the same living, breathing organism, with one purpose, one mission, to win the city title, and we were committed to enjoying ourselves as it happened. The stands rocked with noise and enthusiasm. Fulton Berry, sitting in the middle of the bleachers, stood up and began what had become one of our trademark group cheers, and the whole bleacher section acted as a chorus with a resounding "oh yeah." It was call and response, much in the tradition of the black church and ancestral Africa.

" I got that spirit"
"Oh yeah"
" It's in my heart"
"Oh yeah"
"Goin' tear it apart"
"Oh yeah"
"It's in the air"
"Oh yeah"
"I know it's there"
"Oh yeah"

"It's in my knees"
"Oh yeah"
"Oh help me please"
"Oh yeah"
"It's in my eyes"
"Oh yeah"
"It's in my thighs"
"Oh yeah"
"It's in the street"
"Oh yeah"
"We can't be beat"
"Oh yeah"
"I can't get loose"
"Oh yeah"
"Without my juice"
"Oh yeah"
"It's on the roof"
"Oh yeah"
"A hundred proof"
"Oh yeah"

A round of applause and laughter followed and then someone else started it up again with different verses and we rocked the stands while the team rocked the field and marched to an easy victory. From my new vantage point, the team looked invincible again.

Time, it seemed, had taken it on its own to make the events of my senior year move at a much faster pace than usual. The football season was rolling by, and we rocked the stands each and every game. It was becoming a glorious run at the title, and Westinghouse played exceptionally. The addition of new talent like Wes Garnett and Orin Richburg, two outstanding athletes, lent credibility to the notion of the reestablishment of a legendary city league record for years to come. The team was unstoppable, and soon the last game of the season ended with Westinghouse undefeated in city league play. Preparations for the championship game were underway, and the whole school was still reveling in the defeat of Peabody High School during the season, and it had become our time again to sell wolf tickets all over town.

No one could have been happier than Billy Vasser. His dream of playing for a championship team was coming true. The strange ordeal of transferring from Peabody in the very year that Peabody would beat Westinghouse and go on to win the city title was behind him. The team had redeemed itself, and the road to glory was straight ahead. Team practice during the week before the championship game was serious, with particular attention to detail, and all of our ducks appeared to be in a row.

The evening of the championship game arrived and our excitement couldn't have been greater. This was the night we had been waiting for since our loss to Peabody the year before. Seniors on the team also anticipated it with great enthusiasm. It meant the end of practice and all of the extreme physical conditioning, and for scrubs, it meant the end of the beatings, extortion, humiliation, and psychological abuse suffered at the hands of old guys. It meant that they no longer had a nine-o-clock curfew, could date again, and could wear decent clothes to school without fear of having them taken. This was the ritual of completion, the high ceremony of ambition for The Cult of the Imaginary Circle and the melding of hearts and minds and bodies for a single purpose.

The glare of stadium lights mixing under unobstructed moonlight diffused an eerie glow, an almost spectral presence, out onto the playing field and as the two teams performed warm-up drills, a chilling breeze blew over the stadium. Although everything seemed so right, something wrong attached itself to the evening, something very wrong joined the spectacle about to take place. But it had been there before, growing like an undetected force about to make its presence known.

From the moment of inception, the clash, the helmet-to-helmet collisions, the speed, the airial dynamics, all led to one conclusion, victory for Westinghouse and the spirit of self-redemption. We partied in the stands to the point of excess and made arrangements to continue. We jubilantly filed out of the stadium while the team was celebrating in the locker room. We all made our way back to the school grounds and continued our celebration until the rocking team bus joined us. Their addition to the mix took the celebration up several notches for an hour or so until we all had left for home or other party venues. One such venue was only a block or two from school, and a crowd of us meandered there and hung out until parents shut it down for the night.

At home and still wound up like a tightly coiled mattress spring, I climbed into bed and gradually drifted off to a night of fitful sleep. I tossed and turned unaware of a deadly drama taking place only a few blocks from the school.

Billy Vasser, Orin Richburg, and Wesley Garnett, just back from a trip to the Hill District, stepped out of Garnett's car and were immediately attacked by a gang of knife-wielding thugs. One of them had confronted the trio several hours earlier but had been grabbed and thrown aside by Billy Vasser. He had been looking for the three of them ever since, but with five or six knife-wielding reinforcements. Vasser, Richburg and Garnett all managed to free themselves temporarily from the surrounding circle of dangerous butcher knives, switch-blades, and various and sundry deadly weapons, but they were chased and slashed at until Billy Vasser lay bleeding to death in the middle of the street. It was an unbelievable turn of events. The very night that Vasser had realized his dream of playing on a championship winning team ended with the taking of his life by a gang of violent thugs.

But had it all begun so much earlier and was that night the completion of a circle of violence that had begun with the first ritualistic beating of the first scrub. Had The Cult of the Imaginary Circle birthed and fed and nurtured a monster that, while eating away at the humanity of its members, ultimately consumed the life essence of a devotee? It was as though the very thing that made the team so great, so feared, and so revered had come back to collect its reward. Too few saw the correlation. Too few blamed the system of intimidation and fear. Too few saw the chickens coming home to roost.

Cult Of The Imaginary Circle

This beast of The Circle had raised its ugly head many times before, having been conjured up by ritualistic cult violence. Every drop of red blood beaten from the body of every terrified initiate had succored it. As plain as the snarl on the Bulldog Mascot's face, there was no mistaking that it had served us well. It had been there in the huddles. It had been there in every tackle and every first down the team had made on every field of play. It followed us everywhere we went, at first like a puppy and then like a trained hound until it began to lead us, and it led us far beyond what anyone could have imagined. The pain and hurt every scrub endured, each fist thrown and every insult hurled led us deeper and deeper into what truly had become a system of control and dominance. The violence and psychological terror had become institutionalized.

So many unanswered questions remained. Who knew about it, and had it been winked at or even encouraged by the coaching staff or school officials? Had they known the nature and extent of what had been going on? Surely they had heard the rumors like most of the student population had. In fact, rumor and the reputation of The Room was so widely spread among the student population that few dared even walk the corridor leading to its door. How could the coaching staff have been so close to everything that the team was about and yet remain so oblivious to the systematic violence that had become so integral a part of our everyday life? And what about us? We had all been so tight-lipped about what we were going through, hiding it from our parents and explaining away our injuries as being related to football practice. No one could escape responsibility for the institutionalized violence that had engulfed us all. The community and the city of Pittsburgh all shared the blame for allowing it to flourish. We were all accountable singularly and severally.

Violence had exhibited itself in bruises, contusions, lacerations, an occasional broken nose, and a broken jaw here and there. It had become inherently sadistic, including the time that heat balm, (a thick orange paste, which contained chemicals that reacted with the skin to heat it up) was globbed onto an open wound, a gash in the thigh of an obedient scrub.

The fact that no one had taken the school to task or had taken legal action is amazing, but even more incredible is the fact that until now this story, this undercover truth had never been publicly revealed. It is equally amazing and fortuitous that no one had been seriously injured or killed during team rituals. Who knows what would have happened had we gone through with our plans to rebel? Surely harm would have come in the form of serious injury or death. And it would not have ended on that day. The culture and tradition would have required retribution and satisfaction of all scores until one side had been vanquished.

It was more difficult to believe that Billy Vasser would die on the very night we had won the city championship again after losing it the year before to the school he had transferred from. This truth could not have seemed more like fiction. But we had still not understood the terrible reality that too often violence consumes both victim and perpetrator and creates havoc in the lives of family and friends of each.

Word of Billy Vasser's death spread like wildfire through out the community, and soon my phone jumped off of the hook with the terrible news of what had happened. The team and other supporters gathered early the next morning to confer and get the details. On the one hand, we were numb with disbelief, but on the other, we were insane with anger and desire for revenge. Truckloads and carloads of football players had already been combing the streets and alleys for the culprits. We began walking five and six deep searching for the perpetrators. Fortunately, the police apprehended the murderer before we could have. The result of which would have meant several more lives lost in the streets or wasting away in jail for years to come.

The community remained in shock, and the school was almost paralyzed with angst over what had transpired and what was yet to come. All of the adults in our lives stressed calm, and counseled and admonished us against the need to prove how tough we still were. The community mourned Billy Vasser like a fallen hero, and the funeral services were packed with family, friends, and supporters. It was one of the saddest days in the life of our tight-knit group and an impossible day for the Vasser family. It took weeks to pass before any of us could settle down to normalcy, but the emotional scar tissue was clearly visible and would remain a part of the history of The Cult of the Imaginary Circle.

With just a few months left of my senior year, my thoughts were focused on graduation, college, and the enjoyment of what was left of my final days at Westinghouse. I was pleased with where my relationship with Vonnie was going. We had been together at a couple of parties, and our connection was outstanding. We danced well together and laughed at each other's attempts at humor. And we would be spending more time together because I asked her to the prom and she had said yes.

As time marched, on our senior class made the most of our final days. The lunchroom had become the scene of comedic drama and "almost-out-of-school antics."

On a recurring basis, the Stiggers brothers, James and Alton, performed a routine they called "The Barrel." Their father was a preacher and they had written several parodies of Sunday sermons. These parodies were fashioned after the dynamic and unique sermon delivery style of black preachers that was lyrical but often melodic and contained short and long vocal rhythm patterns that often ended in "ah." The crowning jewel of this style was the voice, a deep, throaty, raspy, reverberating growl. Our lunchroom sermons usually began with James Stiggers pulling us together.

"My brothers and sisters, gather round, gather round. We have some very important words for you this mornin'." Between twenty and thirty of us would pull cafeteria stools together in rows, and we became the church congregation. James would then introduce his brother as Reverend Alton who would raise his hand with his index finger pointing upward and begin, "One daaaaaaaay-ah."

" I was in my kitchen-ah."
"Just ah, washin' my dishes-ah."
"Ah washah washah, ah scrubah scrubah."
THE CONGREGATION: "Preach on, brother, preach on."
"I looked out my window-ah."
"And looked up at the sky-ah."

"The clouds rolled innnn-ah, and the sky turnnnned dark-ah."

"The ground shook mightahly-ah."

"Ah tremble tremble ah, a shake-ah shake-ah."

THE CONGREGATION: "Preach, on brother, preach on."

"Then ah, the clouds opened up-ah."

"Lightning flashed-ah."

"And then I saw The Barrel-ah just ah-shakin'."

"Ah-shake-ah shake-ah."

"And then-ah, I said-ah and then-ah."

THE CONGREGATION: "Amen brother, Amen."

"And then The Barrel came ah rollin'-ah."

"Ah-rumbley, bumbley, tumbley."

"It rolled down the street-ah."

"Rolled in my yard-ah"

"Ah smashed up my hedges-ah."

"Ah-smash-ah, smash-ah."

"It knocked down my kitchen door-ah."

"Broke up all my dishes-ah."

"Rolled up my chest-ah, swisssssh-ah."

"And then it turned-ah and rolled out my kitchen-ah."

"And rumbled down the street-ah, ah-rumbley, bumbley, tumbley."

"My brothers and sisters-ah"

"The Barrel changed my life-ah."

"Made me a better man-ah."

THE CONGREGATION: "Amen, brother, amen."

"Now-ah, I want you to be ready. I said I want you to be ready."

"Because-ah, because-ah."

"One day- ah."

"And it won't be long-ah."

"The Barrel is gonna come ah-rollin-ah."

"I said it won't be long-ah."

THE CONGREGATION: "Amen, brother, amen."

"The Barrel is gonna roll up your body-ah, and roll down your troubles-ah."

THE CONGREGATION: "Preach, brother, preach."

"The Barrel is gonna come ah-rollin'-ah."

"Ah-rumbley, bumbley, tumbley."

And then the bell rang signaling an end to lunch, and we all clapped and laughed as we broke up to go back to class. As we exited the lunchroom and headed down the hallway. Alton Stiggers, walking in front of us, held up his index finger and said in a reverberating tone, "One daaaay ah," and in unison we replied "And it won't be long."

Our senior class was tight, and we were beginning to have almost too much fun. It was a bit ironic that the nearer to the last day we would spend together, the closer we became. Each day I spent away from the influence of the ritualistic Imaginary Circle was a day in the light of an emerging personality. I was becoming more garrulous and outgoing even as I was continuing to look inward at who and what I had been, at who and what I was and at who and what I might become later in life.

I was carrying some emotional baggage and scar tissue from my experience with the Circle Cult, in addition to the mental and physical toughness I had gleaned from the same association. At the age of fourteen and fifteen to have been intimidated and to have felt fear to the point of almost urinating on myself and to have returned to the same terrifying venue day after day etched manly character on my boyish soul. To have participated in physical conditioning to the point of shivering exhaustion without giving in to my body's limitations created a rough physique and incredible stamina. And to have shared it all with a bunch of guys who felt and feared and endured equally created immeasurable camaraderie and respect and regard for one another that would last a lifetime.

I was truly a work in progress, and the more I progressed, the more work I needed. I was becoming enamored with the whole concept and idea of being perceived as a cool individual. I wasn't sure who or what I would become, but I was determined to be chilly. I looked to older paragons of hippness in Homewood for insight and clues on just what cool was all about.

There was one individual of classic proportion, who was the quintessence of coolness. Someone who once had premeditated every move and action but had become cool personified. Cool Scott, as he was known, had become the benchmark for all who subscribed to the doctrine of cool. He wore sunglasses inside and outside, day and night, rain or shine. If caught in a sudden downpour, he was too cool to run through the rain but instead just tilted his head downward and sideways a few degrees so that the water rolled effortlessly off of the brim of his hat. Cool Scott's walk was uncompromisingly stealthy. Alley cats on soft paw pads mimicked his gate and his slowly spoken, smoothly metered,

"Hey baby, what's happenin," iced hot summer air.

There would be plenty of time for me to be made into the man I would eventually become but, for the time being, I was happy to be a part of the rich cultural landscape of Homewood, dotted by individuals like Cool Scott and girls with names like Stuff.

THE END

EPILOGUE

Westinghouse High School was legendary in the city of Pittsburgh and South Western Pennsylvania from the late 1940s through the mid-1960s winning sixteen out of nineteen city high school championships. It was a powerhouse and a great source of pride, achieving mythical proportions: thus The Cult of the Imaginary Circle. Many have debated how and why the success was achieved and several theories have emerged. Some credit great coaching, others cite incredible talent, and a very definitive group asserts that the tight-fisted protocols of the "The Room," were solely responsible for the team's dominance. There is however the possibility that it could have been a combination of all three.

The answer may never be known, yet the debate rages on. So many things have changed that have contributed to the decline of the football dynasty of Westinghouse High School. The coaching staff is entirely different, the pool of talent the school draws from has changed, and the violent system of player control and manipulation no longer exists.

The dynamics of city football that allowed for such a powerhouse to exist may never be the same again. Regardless of who is right, the facts still remain. It was a glorious reign, a yet unbroken record that may stand for eons.

Those of us who played and sacrificed remember the pain and the pleasure and still revel in the myth. Those were times we loved, and those were times we hated. But we chose to endure and to wear our team membership like a badge of merit.

Although the system of player control no longer exists at Westinghouse, hazing and initiation rites involving young people are still in existence all over this country. Some of them have resulted in serious physical and psychological harm to our youth, and some have even led to the tragic death of young initiates. It is incumbent upon parents and guardians to not only know their children but to investigate their schools and extra-curricular activities and anyone and anything their children are involved with to the point of their personal satisfaction and comfort. That may sound like a bit too much but there can never be too much caution with the stewardship of the lives of our progeny who themselves will assume the role of progenitor, most often in our fashion.

What you have read in this book happened back in the 1960s when everyone blindly trusted schools, sports programs, and basically every public institution. That was too much trust then and, in the world we live in now, it should be considered taboo. Paranoia in measured amounts where our children are concerned is not only a good thing but an absolutely necessary thing.

ABOUT THE AUTHOR

Akmed Khalifa was born in Pittsburgh, Pennsylvania and raised in a traditionally valued African American family. His father was born in Pennsylvania, his mother in Louisiana. Their lineage draws from Freedmen that fought in the Civil War and ancestors who struggled to survive the ravages of slavery.

This is Akmed's first published book. Much of the impetus for it came from his concerns, like most Americans, for the safety of our children. He has worked extensively with at risk youth and young people in a variety of public school settings and has been a member of the board of directors of numerous community organizations that address their needs. Akmed has been a frequent volunteer with organizations serving youthful populations. He senses the harm endangering today's youth and recognizes the swirling violence that threatens them and our very way of life. His book makes the point that communities must face this pandemic and overcome it to make the future safe for our progeny and our world.